WACKY NATION

JAMES BAMBER and SALLY RAYNES

WACKY NATION

50 UNBELIEVABLE DAYS OUT AT BRITAIN'S CRAZIEST CONTESTS

ICON BOOKS

Originally published in the UK in 2008 by Icon Books Ltd

This edition published in the UK in 2009 by
Icon Books Ltd, Omnibus Business Centre,
39–41 North Road,
London N7 9DP
email: info@iconbooks.co.uk
www.iconbooks.co.uk

Sold in the UK, Europe, South Africa and Asia
by Faber & Faber Ltd, Bloomsbury House,
74–77 Great Russell Street, London WC1B 3DA or their agents

Distributed in the UK, Europe, South Africa and Asia
by TBS Ltd, TBS Distribution Centre, Colchester Road
Frating Green, Colchester CO7 7DW

This edition published in Australia in 2009
by Allen & Unwin Pty Ltd,
PO Box 8500, 83 Alexander Street,
Crows Nest, NSW 2065

Distributed in Canada by
Penguin Books Canada,
90 Eglinton Avenue East, Suite 700,
Toronto, Ontario M4P 2YE

ISBN: 978-184831-062-9

Typesetting in 10pt New Baskerville by Marie Doherty
Printed and bound in the UK by Clays of Bungay

CONTENTS

ABOUT THE AUTHORS

James Bamber and Sally Raynes, creators of the website www.wackynation.com, lead mundane office lives, but every weekend they unleash their crazy side as they bid to become a World Champion in something silly, or just look silly in a daft contest.

Between them, they have held the World Russian Egg Roulette title, and won silver in 2006's World Snail Racing Championships. In the same year, Sally claimed second place in the World Nettle Eating (women's event), having devoured 34 feet of nettles, and in 2008 was just one second away from becoming a world champion in the Mountain Bike Bog Snorkel. They live in Tiverton, Devon and have aspirations of becoming the wackiest people on the planet. When they're not taking part in wacky events, they can probably be found swimming in the sea!

ACKNOWLEDGEMENTS

We could write a whole book on acknowledgements alone, so would like to thank everybody we have met over the last three years at the wacky events who have kindly assisted us with information, tips and quotes. This includes all the pub landlords and organisers of the events, and the many officials and stewards who have overwhelmed us with information.

Apologies are due to those we harassed over the phone or via email for last-minute facts. We hope we haven't done any event a disservice, and have managed to convey the atmosphere and excitement that we ourselves experienced. We would like to single out Anne Tattersall at the The Big Sheep in Devon for allowing us to photograph her sheep, which proudly appear on the front cover.

We would like to personally mention Eileen Bamber and Jenny and Don Raynes, who checked our work, offered advice and provided regular praise which kept us both motivated when we felt like throwing in the towel (and no, that's not a wacky event). Thank you also to Icon Books for taking on our book and putting up with our constant rants and raves, and a special thank you to Lucy Leonhardt for reading our email and spotting the book's potential.

A final mention also to fellow aficionados of wacky contests: Susie Brown, Dave Brewis, Dave Painter, Hugh Hornby, Peter Holme, Emma Wood, Joel Hicks, Emma-Jayne Hagerty and Mark Rye (the Welsh posse), Steve Preston (aka Stupid Steve), and Jerry and Gwyn Brocklehurst. Plus all the other camera crews and photographers we have met.

Take care where you park

 Injuries possible if you participate

 Spare/warm clothing recommended

 Food and drink available

 Advance applications required to take part or spectate

 Not ideal for small children/babies

 Not ideal for dogs

 Early arrival recommended. Be late and you'll miss it

 Check date/time before you set off

Spectator Fun:

★   30 minutes is enough

★★★★★   You'll never want to leave

Wackiness: *Our own judgement on how wacky the event is*

★   Still fun

★★★★★   Absolute madness

World Champion:

★   Everybody has a chance

★★★★★   Locals or experts usually win, but you never know!

Pain Factor:

★   Pack the Elastoplasts

★★★★★   Health insurance recommended

Training Required:

★   Beginner's luck

★★★★★   Plan a six-month training regime or you'll suffer!

Family Friendly:

★   Definitely one for the brave and stupid

★★★★★   Pram- and zimmer frame-friendly.

It all started with a moment of spontaneity, changing our lives irreversibly. While visiting friends in deepest Wales we had time to thrill, when we were drawn to a small column in the travel section of the newspaper which mentioned a World Championship Bog Snorkelling contest, of all things. We both liked snorkelling and getting dirty, admittedly in sunnier climes, and figured the prospect of becoming World Champions was too irresistible. A few days later, eschewing a trip to the shops, we were standing alongside a 60-foot trench surrounded by colourful eccentrics, the plain mad and a few bewildered sheep, thinking to ourselves, 'You've got to be kidding!'

Watching each competitor plunge into the bog left everyone in hysterics, even though we stood petrified and half contemplated a hasty retreat to the safe haven of our car and maybe that prosaic option of a shopping trip after all. But once it was our turn, we never looked back (we couldn't even if we'd wanted to). A flipper was lost; we swallowed things that should never be swallowed and failed in our bid to become World Champions, but that wasn't the point.

The ethos, as we later realised, isn't about winning, but about 'just taking part, no matter whether you come first, filthy or last'. Challenging ourselves at something completely out of the ordinary was deeply satisfying, leaving an indelible impression on both of us, and an insatiable appetite for more of the same. Who would have thought a wet weekend up to your armpits in mud could ever be fun!

For days afterwards, we were on a high, wandering around in a wondrous state, while finding yet more bog weed in our hair. Out of curiosity we began to research other stupid and daft events. First, the usual suspects popped up: Cheese Rolling, Shin Kicking, Hen Racing, Bognor Birdman and Elephant Throwing (OK, the last one doesn't exist … yet). But we wanted to keep on digging, and every day we boasted to each other, 'There's a Clog Cobbing Contest … whatever that is', or, 'You're not going to believe this, but Wigan have a World Pie Eating Contest!' Within weeks, we had amassed over 150 wacky races, contests, traditions and championships, and were dumbfounded.

Obviously, with no other definitive guide to British wacky events, the ultimate wacky bible (and website) was crying out for someone to take it on and expose the reader to events they never even knew existed. Having spent our childhoods and part of adult life naively believing that theme parks, zoos, arcades and a week in the Costa del Sol (well maybe not) are the be-all and end-all, we thought the book would offer a real alternative for those with the adventure and imagination to dip their toes into something completely different.

So what constitutes wacky? The dictionary defines wacky as, 'crazy, mad or eccentric', derived from the word 'whacky', from the notion of 'being whacked on the head too many times', which probably explains a few things! Our own definition of a wacky event is 'a tradition, contest or race that is bizarre, mad, crazy, stupid, loony, weird, downright foolish or strange, and which elicits responses of "You must be mad" or "You're pulling my leg", when telling other people all about it'.

Childish pastimes (conkers, pea shooting) merit inclusion, as do age-old sporting traditions. Suffice it to say that throwing contests are allowed as long as the object thrown is stupid (clogs, peas, black puddings). Fast and furious contests, the epitome of wackiness, are in abundance, but only for the experienced! Even a game of cricket makes it into the book, but before anyone says that cricket is anything but wacky, there are ridiculous circumstances for its inclusion.

As you will find out when reading our book, there are clusters around Britain that have more than their fair share of wacky events, and other areas where wackiness has not yet penetrated. Gloucestershire, Derbyshire and Devon are Meccas for odd things to do, while the big cities have a severe deficit. London, considering its population of nutters, and the Home Counties are shamefully under-represented. What does that say? Obviously, people in the countryside are more exciting and eccentric and know how to have a good time without forking out money!

Geography isn't the only quirk in the book. The majority of wacky events take place from May to October, and on every weekend of those six months there is at least one wacky thing to do (there are days when you can even take part in two wacky events, provided you break the speed limit).

The beauty of every event is that anyone can take part (apart from a couple exclusively for locals) and watch, no matter how good or bad you are. Unbridled frivolity, a festival atmosphere and a charitable cause are just three reasons why you should go to these contests. In fact, for those who could never make the school football team, now is your chance to shine in a ball game like no other; or maybe if you were never any good at javelin throwing, chucking a pea may be more your forte. There are even entries that will rekindle your love-to-hate relationship with cross-country.

All the events have their own appeal: some have the adrenalin rush, others are just so ridiculous that you spend the entire day laughing your head off, pinching yourself to make sure it's not all a drug-induced dream. Nearly all of them have a rich and unusual history, interesting/completely off the wall characters, and a fair share of over-competitive participants. The events are for absolutely anyone. You will find posses of would-be World Champions obsessively heading around the country, determined to become the best in the world ... at dry foam throwing or pea shooting. Then there is the obverse: groups who strive to look the most daft and insane. Every demographic group is represented, from six-year-old prodigies to 70-year-old grannies. Such parity does not exist at your average championship or contest.

Since our first moment of madness, we have been to all four corners of Britain to discover and fully experience an assortment of over 70 wacky events (and we're not even halfway through our list). Some of our experiences have led to us chasing worms across a field, taking part in a bizarre combat sport in the Cotswolds ... twice, and even competing against a dog in an eating contest.

James has walked away with a World Championship in Russian Egg Roulette, was out-munched in the Mince Pie Eating Contest (well, only by twelve pies) and was completely thrashed in the World Winter Swimming Championships, despite a tight start with the parade of trunks! Sally came close to superstardom with second place in both Nettle Eating and Snail Racing. Sally also had the audacity to put herself forward as the first-ever female entrant in the 2008 Shin Kicking Championships. Unfortunately, no other female combatants were forthcoming and officials incredibly entered Sally into the men's draw. Oddly, she refused to take any further part, but we believe she has become the first-ever

Women's Champion by default? Sally will defend her 'title' next year in high heels! She even entered the Gurning, but unfortunately the judges disqualified her for being too professional. We have also courted much controversy over the last year or so, including a near-decapitation in the Stone Skimming Championship, walking away from the Marbles Championships with bleeding knuckles, and suffering the embarrassment of our hen receiving a red card in the Hen Racing, all of which has been broadcast on various television shows around the world.

On a more serious note, the events in the book (and others) can suddenly disappear without warning, never to return. Over the past decade, many have been abandoned or cancelled due to a variety of reasons, while some face an annual battle with insurance or the elements to go ahead. The World Biscuit Throwing Contest, the Stroud Brick and Rolling Pin Throwing Championship, and the Adur Bath Tub Race are three such victims that deserve to continue, if only for their title to raise a few chuckles. The world-famous Toe Wrestling Contest has reached an impasse because no one is mad enough to run it, or maybe the feet in Derbyshire are just too smelly! Every year, health and safety fears come closer to sounding the death knell for the Cheese Rolling and Tar Barrels, while the World Conker Championship faces the looming threat of climate change. Tradition is hard to end, but one day even the hardiest and most vehemently supported events may succumb. Go today before they all fall by the wayside!

We have provided contact details for as many of the events as possible, but given the last-minute and chaotic shenanigans of some, we direct you to our website, www.wackynation.com, as the first point of reference. At the time of going to press, the costs, venue and date relate to the 2008 calendar, and it's conceivable that details in future years will change.

Finally, some words of caution. Officials do their utmost to ensure that every event is safe to watch or participate in, but some can be physically demanding and, of course, a few involve alcohol. To avoid a trip home in an ambulance or arriving at an event utterly unprepared, we have produced an at-a-glance guide at the start of each event to help you decide which ones are suitable for you. We have also indicated which events require training beforehand, and also the likelihood that a newcomer could become a World Champion.

We also hope that the tried-and-tested tips section will be of use, preparing you for a shot at the World Championship or at least giving the bare minimum advice to avoid becoming a laughing-stock. Just don't do too well or you may upset the locals!

Until you take part you will never really understand the liberation felt when caked in mud from head to foot, indulging in childish pastimes, running full-pelt down a hill after a lump of cheese, or jumping into an ice-cold sea just because it's Christmas Day. But we promise, once you start, you won't stop.

Having dedicated our lives to wackiness and now believing we are the authority (at least in Britain for the moment), it was only a matter of time before we took on our own contest, and we hope to add one more event to the wacky calendar in 2009.

www.wackynation.com

We may have spent many years cataloguing events, but we are convinced that there are still more mad and crazy races, contests and traditions out there. Please get in touch via our website or email us at wackynation@hotmail.com and let us know what they are (no matter how small), so that we can share the lunacy. Or alternatively, look out for our orange T-shirts at the events.

WORLD NETTLE EATING CHAMPIONSHIP

'A contest for gastronomic gladiators'

Location: Bottle Inn, Marshwood, Crewkerne, Dorset. Marshwood is about five miles along the B3165 off the A35 near Lyme Regis

Date: The Saturday before the summer solstice (21 June)

Time: Registration from 5.30pm, begins 6.30pm

Entry fee: £1 (includes free T-shirt)

Further information: www.thebottleinn.co.uk

Grid reference: SY 378 997

Spectator Fun:	★★
Wackiness:	★★★
World Champion:	★★★
Pain Factor:	★★★★
Training Required:	★★★★
Family Friendly:	★★★

$($ **WHAT HAPPENS** $)$

Competitors have one delicious hour to munch through as many nettle stalks as possible, and whoever manages to strip the most bare, without being sick, will be declared the winner (or should that be loser?).

An array of characters – seasoned locals, foolhardy students and the plain stupid – are here to prove they have the mettle to become World Champion. Seated on a purpose-built stage within the beer garden of the Bottle Inn, and within 'throwing up' distance of the crowd, competitors examine their meal as officials dish out the first batches of stalks, each one about two feet in length with over twenty tasty leaves. Those new to the contest are perhaps afforded a last opportunity to drop out before attempting the unknown, as doubts run riot in their minds: How badly will the nettles sting? Do I have to eat all my greens? Who will get my beers?

For some entrants these questions will be answered sooner than they hoped.

Many remain unfazed, preferring to carry on smoking, drinking beer or emptying their bladder in readiness for the contest. Before the start, officials remind the entrants of the rules, including remaining in their seat for the whole hour and, as far as the eating goes, devouring every single leaf, even the ones looking suspiciously dark-coloured. Luckily, the seeds can be left on the stalk.

There is a hesitant start for many virgin nettle-eaters, preferring a cautious approach and opting to delicately pluck the leaves and tease their lips. The competitors who have entered before, and should know better, adopt a more ruthless approach – diving in, ripping the leaves off and applying their own personal technique to rolling the leaves into an edible size. Requests for more nettles from the early leaders follow very quickly, while those coping less favourably soon realise that five stalks will probably be more than enough.

For the uninitiated, the taste is very bland, like lettuce leaves but with unsavoury additives such as bird muck, and novices may well find it tricky to keep the nettles down; the first disgorgement inevitably occurs within the first fifteen minutes.

Beyond the opening 30 minutes of frenetic munching, the pace subsides as competitors begin to feel the effects of their labour, often regretting setting an over-eager pace. Tongues begin to blacken, cheeks puff out, jawbones ache and the same gooey mass of nettles that has been chewed for the last five minutes will not go down. This is the point where the strugglers either leave voluntarily or face dismissal for breaking one of the rules, as competitors' bladders bulge under the strain of copious drinking. The risk of vomiting is always lurking behind every mouthful and there is a look of disappointment on the faces of competitors who were progressing very nicely but were caught out by an involuntary waterfall-like spew, much to the delight of the cameras.

Inside the final five minutes and it's not only the nettles that have well and truly wilted. One by one, entrants drop out of the contest, and those who remain – usually less than a quarter – have succumbed to the wretchedness of the whole contest but stubbornly remain seated, picking off leaves and pretending to eat while maintaining an impressive gurn, consoled by the pride of remaining till the very bitter end.

Only the main contenders continue to gorge themselves, and officials keep the crowd informed of the leaders and losers. The finish is anti-climactic but much welcomed, as competitors race off to the nearest toilet – in no mood for celebration or an encore.

Even if you make it through to the end grudgingly refusing to vomit, there is no antidote available to relieve the lingering pain, the numbed fingertips and the foul taste of bird droppings. Only an excess of beer – which is fortunately the prize for the winners – will help the contestants through the remainder of the weekend, while a reliable memory reminds them never to enter again, although many do come back more determined to improve on their paltry performance.

HISTORY

First conceived as the longest stinging nettle contest, the event evolved following a pub argument between two farmers back in 1986. Both farmers declared that they had the longest stinging nettle on their land, leading to one of them, Alex Williams, bringing a fifteen-foot nettle stalk into the pub and stupidly declaring that he would eat any stalk that was bigger. A few years later, a challenge was laid down to anyone who could eat more nettles than Alex, as an impromptu side show during the pub's summer solstice celebrations. Thus the event was born. The current record stands at a staggering 76 feet of nettles, and the record holder has vowed to return to the competition should his efforts ever get surpassed.

Many contestants have resorted to cheating, including two local policemen who one year attempted to stuff the uneaten leaves into their clothes, but they were soon spotted by the nettle police. Others have tried stealing their neighbours' bare stalks, applied cream to ease the sores, or numbed the mouth using hot chilli oil.

ESSENTIALS

Arrive early to register because there will be a limit of around 60 entrants, with people actually queuing up to eat nettles! Entry forms are available on the day from the pub on a first-come basis. Only nettles provided by the organisers are eaten and there are several rules to the competition, including automatic disqualification for anyone who regurgitates the nettles or eats anything else during the contest, i.e. any mouth-numbing substances. Officials will spot any foul play as they pace around the arena on the look-out for potential cheats, vomiters, or a suspicious pile of nettle leaves under a competitor's chair.

There is a car park and basic campsite with toilets to the rear of the pub for a small fee (£5 per person, including a lovely beer glass), and the contest is part of a weekend-long beer festival with live bands.

TIPS

The winner in 2007 admitted he had practised religiously for two weeks beforehand, acquiring the taste and exercising the jaw muscles ahead of one hour of intensive mastication. However, for the majority who prefer to limit themselves to one day of pain, the best advice is to tear off several leaves at once and then roll them into a tight ball using the palms, before laboriously chewing and swallowing. Soaking the leaves in the beer may also improve the nettles' palatability. Lasting the full hour may depend on how enthusiastically you begin the contest, but the key is keeping the throat as moist as possible, with additional water provided by the organisers.

BEFORE YOU ENTER

… It's said that nettles are a very good laxative!

IF YOU LIKE THIS

Try the Onion Eating at the Newent Fayre in September, but if you fancy a more tasty challenge, head off to Wigan, Greater Manchester for the World Pie Eating Championships (see page 232), which is held every December in Harry's Bar. This was originally a contest of who could devour the most meat pies (seven in three minutes, before anyone asks), but in 2006, after protests from healthy-eating lobbyists, the event instead became the fastest pie eating contest.

SHIN KICKING CHAMPIONSHIPS

'Kick as hard as you can, but leave those steel toe-capped boots behind!'

Location:	Dover's Hill, Chipping Campden, Gloucestershire
Date:	First Friday after Whitsun
Time:	From 7pm
Entry Fee:	Free
Further information:	www.olimpickgames.co.uk
Grid reference:	SP 136 395

Spectator Fun:	★★★★
Wackiness:	★★★★★
World Champion:	★★★★
Pain Factor:	★★★★★
Training Required:	★★★★
Family Friendly:	★★★

WHAT HAPPENS

Deep in the Cotswolds is probably the last place you would expect to find an ancient tradition that combines the oriental pursuits of sumo wrestling and karate to produce the ultimate example of wacky sadomasochism. Shin kicking is the sport of kicking your opponent's shins in a series of bouts until one or both of you drop to the floor in agony ... and they think cock fighting is barbaric!

The Shin Kicking contest takes place beside Dover's Hill, in an arena fit for gladiators. Watched by thousands of spectators, the few naive competitors who dare to take part are paired off in the opening round, often very unfairly, regardless of height, girth or shoe size. This often means some real David and Goliath contests, but here the outcome is always going to favour Goliath!

Competitors first frantically stuff as much straw as possible up the front of their trousers to pad their shins, transforming even the skinniest legs into bulging tree stumps, while those dressed in shorts turn cissy and make excuses before hastily exiting the arena. One competitor bravely, or stupidly, declines all forms of shin protection, but at least he doesn't have the arrogance to fight in a pair of sandals. Sensibly, footwear is restricted to soft trainers and shoes; steel toe-capped boots are definitely not allowed, but only if someone complains.

Contestants, dressed in traditional white shepherd coats or smocks, stride manfully into the arena. Some, however, could be mistaken for scarecrows with straw billowing out from their trousers, giving the impression that they have an entire bale stuck up one trouser leg (some often do).

The contest begins with competitors squaring up to each other, sporting frightened expressions, before grabbing hold of each other's lapel and staring one another out. Upon the referee's shout, they begin furiously kicking their opponent's shins while still maintaining a grip on each other; the close contact prevents either opponent from running away.

The pace can be fast and furious as the competitors shuffle around the muddied arena while unleashing random kicks, often managing one kick every second. Competitors take turns attacking, and the play moves back and forth, often menacingly towards the crowd. It looks incredibly painful, and although the shins are protected, there can be only so much relentless tibia-bashing before some bruising is incurred; kicks are deviously aimed towards the back of the legs, or hard enough to penetrate the straw padding, landing directly on the bone with an excrutiating thud accompanied by much whimpering.

A bout is won when one competitor has received enough brutality and is thrown down by his opponent (or falls down on purpose), provided he makes at least one successful kick first. If both competitors fall, then the first to hit the ground loses the bout, and any kick above the knee results in the bout going the other way. Aside from these minor rules, you can kick as much and as hard as you like. Screaming is not allowed! The referee, who is called a stickler, makes sure all rules are followed and indicates which competitor won the bout by pointing his stick.

There are sometimes more tactical, slower contests where competitors prefer to bide their time before aiming more kicks, often contorting their body around the opponent to do so. The bout becomes more of a peculiar dance than a combat sport, neither player having the energy or the conviction to take a swipe. The crowd boo the cautious approach by both players – many of them have only come here to witness grown

men squealing, and often encourage a physical battle with shouts of 'Whack him!' or 'Take his legs!'

In desperation there are tired, half-hearted kicks, misdirected and painfully close to more delicate regions, with oohs and aaahs from the crowd, who avert their eyes as they anticipate an agonising climax to the bout. Inevitably, fatigue resolves the contest rather than sheer agony, as both players tire of supporting their opponent's weight and collapse to the ground.

Each game is a knockout and completed within five minutes. The first person to win two bouts takes the match and limps into the next round, where competitors suddenly lose all desire to win and fall down far too easily. The eventual winner receives the grandiose title of British Champion (and probably World Champion, since this is the only such contest in the world) and reluctantly must return the following year to defend his title.

HISTORY

Records date back to 1612, when shin kicking was part of the Cotswold Olimpicks, which included other exciting events such as singlestick (a cross between fencing and stick fighting), wrestling, jumping in sacks and dancing. In the 19th century, shin kicking became more aggressive and it's said that competitors strengthened their shins with coal hammers or iron-tipped boots, often competing in front of crowds of 30,000. It was finally stopped in 1852 and since its most recent revival in 1951, the contest has been toned down, thankfully.

The contest could one day yield an Olympic champion. The Shin Kicking Association of Great Britain put forward an unsuccessful proposal to include the game in the 2012 London Olympics. The association, whose motto is 'If it ain't broke, yer not kickin' hard enough', believes that shin kicking deserves Olympic recognition and in 2012 will celebrate the 400th anniversary of the supposed beginning of the modern Olympiad.

ESSENTIALS

Shin kicking is the main event of the Cotswold Olimpicks, also known as the Dover's Games (named after Robert Dover, the founder of the Olimpicks), and includes the less violent pursuits of the five-mile run, an *It's a Knockout*-style team event and a 'Champion of the Hill' event. The venue also has a variety of fairground rides, stalls and displays. There is a car park provided for a small fee (about £2.50), but it's better to park in Chipping Campden so that you can take part, or hobble, in the torchlight procession at the end of the night back into the town.

TIPS

Don't enter ... this is definitely one we recommend you spectate! The contest will favour those with a rugby player physique, i.e. short, powerful legs, so be prepared for a mauling if you are tall, skinny and averse to any aggression. Stuffing straw up your trouser leg, a clandestine pair of shin pads, and some pre-contest beer will cushion the blows and anaesthetise the pain, but attack is the best form of defence.

To avoid a stalemate, as so many of the bouts inevitably become, there's one very effective technique to winning: turn your opponent to the side as he starts to kick, which will hopefully unbalance him enough to send him over. This tactic is aided by the slippery surface, and many competitors actually fall over without too much assistance, so even a gentle swipe will suffice.

Joe McDonagh, 2005 Champion, divulged proven advice to beat your opponent: 'Obviously you knock the inside of their standing leg away as they are in mid-kick.' Meanwhile, 2008 Champion and experienced backsworder (another ancient and painful village tradition), Steve 'Bulldog' Williams, had a much more simple piece of wisdom: 'Stay on your feet!'

For competitors of a slight build, there is some hope, provided you come through the first match unscathed. The entrants with brute strength and plenty of weight often find themselves completely drained very early on in the evening, offering an opportunity for weaker, but fitter entrants to turn the contest into a test of stamina.

WACKY FACT

Besides the Olimpicks, miners in Lancashire in the 19th century once grappled naked except for their boots, in private bouts of kicking. That is probably why the rules now prohibit any kicks above the knee!

IF YOU LIKE THIS

2007 saw the inaugural World Gravy Wrestling Championships, held in a supermarket car park in Darwen, Lancashire.
A gravy-filled paddling pool provides the bizarre setting for
the traditional wrestling competition involving teams of
three. There are no kicks or punches allowed, but expect the
ladled-out action to come thick and fast.

WORLD WORM CHARMING CHAMPIONSHIPS

'Twang those worms out!'

Location: Willaston County Primary School, Willaston, Nantwich, Cheshire. Off the M6 at Junction 16 and follow signs for Nantwich

Date: The last Saturday in June

Time: 1pm for 2pm start

Entry fee: £3 for a plot and £1 admission

Further information: www.wormcharming.com

Grid reference: SJ 676 526

Spectator Fun: ★★★★

Wackiness: ★★★★★

World Champion: ★★★

Pain Factor: ★

Training Required: ★★★

Family Friendly: ★★★★★

WHAT HAPPENS

Competitors go on the charm offensive as they attempt to lure as many worms out of the ground as possible, using an array of odd and quirky-looking gimmicks in a contest of much twanging and fiddling!

Teams of two are allocated a three-metre square plot and have just 30 slimy minutes to collect their worms. One member of the team, called a 'Gillie', is responsible for handling the worms, while the other concentrates on the more arduous task of worm charming. Teams are equipped with an empty worm pot and their choice of implements. They must also obey several contest rules, notably no application of a drug or stimulant (that includes water) and definitely no digging. Officials patrol the arena, precluding any cheating or devious ploys. Besides the race to charm the most worms, there is also a prize for the heaviest worm, as long as it fits in the worm pot.

The start of the race is chaotic, as teams set out to seek the most productive spot in their plot for charming. The most commonly used method to worm charm is 'twanging'. This involves inserting a garden fork into the soil and then vibrating it, usually with the aid of a piece of wood striking the fork handle (also called 'fiddling'), or vigorously moving the fork back and forth.

Early on, there are shouts across the arena of 'There's a worm!' and 'There's another one!' Gradually the shouts become more frenetic as worms pop up all over the place. A few less fortunate teams are left lamenting their choice of plot, and now and again ask in forlorn hope, 'Is that a worm or a twig?'

Many novice charmers are too generous with their energy and soon realise that 30 minutes of twanging will be hard work. Besides twanging, competitors employ various devices and techniques, some practical and effective, others eccentric and audacious but inevitably useless, all contributing to the cacophony of bangs, thumps and clonks.

Over the years the event has seen tap dancing, an unorthodox use of knitting needles – which unfortunately skewered the worms – and even a pony to hoof the ground, although those charming at the rear end of the pony probably had more to contend with. On the even sillier side, in 2006 one competitor played the double bass, hoping to entice more worms. However hard you coax the worms, music is unlikely to charm them, even if it's in tune.

Into the final few minutes, and dirty tactics come into play as teams begin to snatch worms from the edge of neighbouring plots in an effort to bolster numbers, but this ploy is often spotted by rival teams, who shout back, 'Hands off, that's our worm!'

The end of the charm brings relief to the crowd and the worms who have managed to evade capture. Teams of officials retire to a secluded corner and have the laborious task of counting the number of worms. Any tie-breaks, such as happened just once back in 2003, are then settled with another five minutes of charming on two randomly selected plots, much to the chagrin of the worms.

The winner receives a trophy in the shape of a worm, and don't worry about the captured worms – they are released later in the evening when the birds have flown off. As for the heaviest worm in the contest, perhaps it's kept back as a local delicacy?

HISTORY

The event was conceived as a fundraiser back in 1980, and the record – also set that year – is a staggering 511 worms, which works out at an incredible seventeen worms a minute, and is also a Guinness world record. However, the average number of worms charmed by the winner is usually around 200, which is still an amazing feat. The current record for the heaviest worm is 6.6 grams.

In the past, teams have resorted to idiotic lengths to charm, including dressing up as a bird or bouncing on rubber balls disguised as racehorses. One entrant even went to the sartorial extreme of wearing an inflatable sumo wrestling costume attached with spring-loaded metal shoes; unsurprisingly this method yielded no worms. For future entrants with idiotic ideas, the crux of worm charming is to simulate rain to coax the worms above ground, and not to use methods liable to shock them into a state of trauma or a fit of the giggles! A past winner admitted that he will customise a zimmer frame for future worm charming when old age limits his twanging ability!

One lone competitor has even invented an elaborate device for charming the worms (see photograph below), which on first impressions perhaps belongs in a museum rather than a World Championship.

Finally, there have been suspicions by the counting committee of foul play by some teams who break worms into two or more bits. Luckily, only healthy-looking worms count, with the teams responsible for any acts of cruelty reported to the RSPCW.

ESSENTIALS

There are 144 plots available and the contest takes place in the middle of a school playing field, with a strong local contingent. Plots should be booked in advance, but a small number are redistributed before the start. The event is always well attended, with competitors of all ages and plenty of entertainment on offer including tug of war and dancing displays. There is limited car parking. Finally, this isn't a 'small children charming' event so make sure any sharp tools, e.g. forks, are well protected before you arrive.

TIPS

According to a previous World Champion, 'twanging' and 'plenty of elbow grease and persistence' are the key to winning, but remember to use the fork at a steep angle otherwise you may be disqualified for attempting to dig up the turf. Also, don't forget to wear gloves to prevent blisters. To delay fatigue, it's also permitted for the team members to swap over during the contest, and they can even draft in substitutes, but only two people are allowed in the plot at any one time, although rules are relaxed for very small children.

Don't expect to charm worms straight away; work different areas of the plot until there is some success. There are even rumours that certain areas of the arena are luckier than others – unfortunately the plots are all randomly allocated. Ideally, a central location is most efficacious, providing greater opportunity to receive (or pinch!) worms from neighbouring plots. A final tip is to wait for worms to completely surface before catching. Otherwise an impatient Gillie will see them wiggle out of their slippery grasp back into the soil.

WACKY FACT

The rules of the contest are written in over 30 languages including Tibetan, and, suitably, a competitor one year tried meditation to attract the worms to the surface. No prizes for guessing how many worms this idea managed!

IF YOU LIKE THIS

Try the International Worm Charming Contest in Blackawton, South Devon, a scaled-down contest with around 50 plots, but competed no less fiercely. Teams, with up to three people, have five minutes' charming without picking up the worms and then a further fifteen minutes to collect them. The rules are more relaxed than the World Championships, with the use of water and concoctions permitted, provided the teams are prepared to drink what they charm with. This usually involves a tantalising mixture of tomato ketchup, mustard and Worcester sauce. There is even an official worm cheat, guarding his own patch and enticing fellow competitors away with plenty of sweets.

BOTTLE KICKING AND HARE PIE SCRAMBLE

'It's not just the bottle that gets kicked around'

Location:	Hallaton, Leicestershire
Date:	Easter Monday
Time:	The main game begins at 3pm
Entry fee:	Free
Further information:	www.hallaton.org/bottlekicking.html
Grid reference:	SP 787 965

Spectator Fun:	★★
Wackiness:	★★
Pain Factor:	★★★★
Family Friendly:	★

WHAT HAPPENS

Rival teams from the neighbouring villages of Hallaton and Medbourne engage in a very physical sport, best described as a hybrid of rugby, football and boxing.

Played on a pitch about one mile long in the middle of the countryside, the teams battle it out to get a 'bottle' over their own stream to score a goal. The game is far removed from typical team pastimes, with no limit to the number of players taking part and only one rule. That is there aren't any, including no referees. The passion and energy shown by those who take part makes modern rugby look like a game of netball.

The bottle, which replaces the conventional ball, is an old wooden beer keg, about a gallon in size and not something you want to be on the receiving end of. The contest will see three different kegs brought into the action, two filled with beer and one remaining empty. Earlier in the day, the kegs are blessed in church and then decorated, before being carried at arms' length by some of the players in the procession to the start at Hare Pie Bank.

Once sufficiently warmed up with beer, the players gather for the kick off, dressed appropriately in various rugby shirts, with the Hallaton team made up of locals and Medbourne traditionally, and gratefully, receiving any neutrals to bolster numbers. From an outsider's perspective there are no clues to who belongs to which team, and as the day progresses the fields get muddier, creating farcical conditions and demanding local familiarity of the players.

The battle commences once a local villager has launched the bottle into the air three times. An almighty scramble ensues after the third throw, with one imprudent competitor

catching the bottle and consequently becoming flattened in a rolling mass scrum.

Movement early on is slow and steady as both teams stubbornly refuse to give ground and are patient enough to bide their time, with no significant progress for up to 30 minutes. The bottle eventually breaks loose as one player tries to make a dash for it with the scrum in pursuit, but opposition players come out of nowhere to take him down. The scrum then reforms, and play grinds to a halt, usually resulting in a lengthy impasse.

Besides running with the bottle, there are no restrictions on how the bottle moves, as long as players do not resort to mechanical means. Teams can also throw or kick the bottle, but the latter method is definitely not advisable unless you fancy a broken foot.

Now and again, one of the teams may significantly outnumber the other as players pile in, and as the scrum becomes dangerously unbalanced it's only a matter of time before it collapses under the uneven weight. Groans and shouts soon follow, with limbs poking out in all directions from the massive mound of contorted bodies. At this point, there are cries of 'back up' and everyone immediately moves off (all players are aware of the dangers of the game), allowing those at the bottom to extricate themselves. Many display short-term memory loss and return to the fray minutes later for further punishment or, perhaps, revenge.

The two goals are streams, which mark the far ends of the 'pitch'. Hallaton's goal is a stream near the Berwick Arms, while Medbourne's goal is one mile away. In between there are several fields, barbed wire fences, hedgerows and the odd sheep. The play randomly shifts between the teams from end to end, and the physical barriers are simply ignored as players lose volition and find themselves crashing straight over, whether they want to or not. The other side of the barrier resembles a mini battlefield, with the less fortunate overtaken by the advancing mass of players and electing to dive for cover.

Players tend to drift in and out of the game as tiredness and semi-drunkenness set in, but there are always enough people to keep the game going. The play consequently becomes more open, with a goal increasingly likely. In keeping with similar traditions, there is no restriction on who can take part, but locals are more likely to get a chance to run with the barrel or, worse, get clobbered by the opposition.

As the bottle creeps nearer to one of the two goals, the opposition inevitably acquiesce. It's a long way back from here, and the struggling team would be better off conceding

and starting again. Scoring a goal involves one member of the team running to the other side of the stream and catching the bottle as it flies over the last hedge.

Once the celebrations are over, and this can take quite a while, the players head back to the middle to kick off the second bottle. The contest ends when one village has scored twice, often not happening until late into the evening, and the teams then return to the village centre. Left behind is a trail of destruction, with fences, hedges and walls usually the worse for wear. The final act of the match is for some of the players to climb the Buttercross in the village and toast their victory with a drink from one of the kegs, now containing very frothy beer.

HISTORY

Before the Bottle Kicking there is a parade and a ritual called the 'Hare Pie Scramble', which involves pieces of the pie being thrown to the crowd. For those with a culinary interest, the hare pie contains hare meat, ox liver and forcemeat, and it's probably for the better that the pie is thrown away! The history of the ritual is very hazy, but the story goes that a bull was chasing two local women in a field until a hare ran past and distracted him. In thanks, the ladies donated land to the local church and in return the rector offered the village a sermon and hare pies on Easter Monday.

The first written record of the Bottle Kicking, the Tailby Letter, dates back to 1796, but it's believed to have taken place many years earlier, although back then it was more about the hare pie ritual. Originally the pies and ale were placed in the centre of a ten- by six-yard oblong bank, with the men scrambling for the prizes, which resulted in bloody noses and broken limbs … nothing has changed, then!

Over the years, the contest has seen many protests. Once, local gentry objected to its barbaric nature, only to see the locals react by stampeding over their gardens. The local rector suffered a similar fate when he declared that the match should not continue, because of its supposed pagan origins. The only protest in recent times has come from the ambulance service, who, after witnessing excessive casualties in 2006, requested an end to the Bottle Kicking. But, like other traditions, it will take a lot more than a few broken bones for this immemorial contest to get cancelled permanently.

ESSENTIALS

While there is no referee, marshals surround the field of play to maintain some order and decorum, if that is possible. A few years ago a shortage of marshals created a minor panic in Hallaton until local people volunteered at the last minute.

Unlike other ball games, safe car parking is not an issue, as the game is not expected to stray beyond the confines of the fields. However, the event is very popular, with over 3,000 people attending the game, so arrive early to avoid a long walk. Many years ago, hordes of spectators even arrived by special train for the contest.

TIPS

This is one of the more physical games in the wacky calendar and all those taking part need to be familiar with the safety issues. Every year there are minor injuries, including broken legs and concussion; even the odd spectator or photographer can unwittingly become absorbed into the play. In 2006, one player was standing in the right place at the wrong time as one side were about to score and, inadvertently, the bottle ended up flying into his face, causing a head injury. It's said that many year-long feuds are settled at the Bottle Kicking. As a rule, only the more foolhardy risk playing, and the sight of many competitors drinking copious amounts of beer acts as a warning for the neutrals who fancy joining in. This is one tradition to respect and the action is ideally viewed from a safe distance.

WACKY FACT

About 100 years ago, participants would often wear bowler hats and gaiters, but suitable attire nowadays would be crash helmets and shin pads.

IF YOU LIKE THIS

There are many rugby-type traditional sports held throughout Britain, all with their own quirks and all guaranteed to shoot you with an adrenalin rush (even if you decide only to spectate). The Haxey Hood in Lincolnshire is fought between supporters of four rival pubs across two local villages, and the match is officiated by twelve boggins and a fool! The players battle to sway the hood (carry a leather cylinder) into their favourite hostelry to win the match, which unfortunately for the spectators can take several hours.

For more rough and tumble, where even the referee is too afraid to turn up, try the Workington Uppies and Downies game in Cumbria, held three times over the Easter period. First played back in the 18th century, in this game the pitch is approximately two miles wide, and teams attempt to manoeuvre a leather ball either to a water- or land-based goal. In between there are various man-made and natural hazards, which can add considerable area to the pitch, and over the years, unbridled enthusiasm among the teams has sadly seen several drownings. This is one game definitely not for the faint-hearted.

WORLD PEA THROWING CHAMPIONSHIPS

'Easy-peasy'

Location:	Lewes Arms, Mount Place (off the High Street), Lewes, East Sussex
Date:	A Sunday in October
Time:	2pm registration for 3pm start
Entry fee:	£1 for three throws
Further information:	Lewes Arms, 01273 473152
Grid reference:	TQ 414 102

Spectator Fun:	★
Wackiness:	★★
World Champion:	★★★★
Pain Factor:	★
Training Required:	★★
Family Friendly:	★★★

WHAT HAPPENS

Muscles can be left behind for this throwing contest but don't forget your binoculars, as a bird's-eye view of the competition is the best way for seeing where your pea lands!

Competitors select three peas from a rapidly defrosting bag of frozen peas and then hurl them, either by throwing or flicking, down the alleyway, all within one minute. A variety of techniques are employed, with most competitors adopting either the javelin technique, taking a small run up followed by a lob, or choosing the under-arm method and preferring to throw with accuracy rather than power. Either way, the contestant will scan the horizon after their throw, trying to catch sight of a tiny green speck. Other methods of throwing the pea are not permitted, and the rules, as listed on the wall of the pub, state that kicking, spitting or blowing are not allowed ... we assume they are still referring to the peas.

Unlike the majority of throwing contests, the distance is measured from where the pea finally comes to rest after interminably rolling down the street, and not the first contact with the ground. This is probably a good thing because the peas often ricochet off the buildings or disappear in mid-flight, finishing up in a gutter or eventually trickling down off the rooftops. Thankfully, peas are immediately declared void should they vanish down drains, come to a halt under a car, or be abused by animals.

The narrow throwing arena soon becomes littered with green smudges and, due to the small size and colour of the projectile, chaos often ensues as the officials dispute which pea has just been thrown. Often the wrong one will end up getting measured, but no one really notices. To add to the confusion, competitors must stand by their best pea after their throw, further congesting the alleyway, while children chase the peas, usually finishing up in a mini-squabble.

Perhaps aimed at the children more than the adults, a final contest rule requests that no batting, slapping or punching is permitted! The use of frozen peas adds further amusement, due to the thawing effect – maybe the event should be renamed the World Mushy Pea Throwing Contest!

HISTORY

The Lewes Arms is over 220 years old, but the pea throwing has been going only since 1998. Apparently the idea came from a hard-of-hearing local in the pub mishearing a conversation and exclaiming, 'Pea Throwing!' The current records are 44 metres for men and 28.5 metres for the ladies, but no one will ever know whether the right pea was measured.

ESSENTIALS

Luckily, no one challenges the decisions made in what has become a very family-orientated contest. The winners usually receive a bottle of wine or chocolates, but the laid-back approach does make a mockery of its World Championship status.

The contest lasts about one hour, but because of its low-key nature competitors will need to make themselves known to officials beforehand. The event is open to children of all ages, ladies and men. Apart from the throwing, not much else goes on except for copious drinking and eating at the public house (just don't order mushy peas with your evening meal). However, if you hang around all year, the Lewes Arms offers an eclectic array of entertainment including an annual pantomime in an upstairs room of the pub and a spaniel race, which other animals can enter, if cunningly disguised as a spaniel.

The pub even hosts the obscure sport of Dwile Flonking, where flonkers, snurds, swadgers and wantons are commonplace and game rules make pea throwing sound positively normal. In turn, every player (the flonker) in the team flonks the dwile (an ale-soaked dishcloth), attached to the driveller (a long stick), at the opposing team who surround the flonker in a circle. The aim is to hit one player of the opposition with the dwile, and points are awarded for where on the body is hit, but if they miss there is the penalty (or should that be prize?) of drinking ale. Every player in the team has a turn in the middle. Points are also lost at the end for any players left sober ... and, as you may have already guessed, the point of the game is not winning, but getting drunk. The Lewes Arms is definitely a candidate for the wackiest public house.

TIPS

The contest allows the use of frozen peas only, rather than the dried pea variety, which is bad news, particularly for competitors who throw last and are faced with a soggy missile to hurl. To combat this problem, select your peas just before it's your turn, or you could always resort to cheating and coat the pea with nail varnish!

Under-arm throwing is perhaps more advantageous, providing the pea with greater rolling opportunity and reducing the likelihood of hitting the buildings. Finally, keep one eye on where the pea has landed, or you may inherit somebody else's efforts and inadvertently become World Champion.

WACKY FACT

Organisers in the past even resorted to organic peas in the mistaken belief that because they contained fewer impurities they would be more aerodynamic.

IF YOU LIKE THIS

For pea-brains who can't get enough, there is also the World Pea Shooting Championships, held in Witcham, Cambridge-shire (see page 102), which will appeal to anyone with a penchant for regressing to their childhood.

BONSALL WORLD CHAMPIONSHIP HEN RACING

'Batteries not included!'

Location:	Barley Mow pub, Bonsall, near Matlock, Derbyshire
Date:	First Saturday in August
Time:	From 2pm
Entry fee:	£1

Further information:
www.barleymowbonsall.co.uk

Grid reference:	SK 275 580

Spectator Fun:	★★★★
Wackiness:	★★★
World Champion:	★★
Pain Factor:	★
Training Required:	★★★★
Family Friendly:	★★★★★

WHAT HAPPENS

Taking place in the palatial surroundings of the pub car park, hens unknowingly compete in a series of heats over a distance of 30 feet with the winners progressing through to the final, although racing is probably the last thing on the hens' minds.

The heats begin with a brief parade of the hens before the crowd, with the owners maintaining a very tight grip. Hens are then lined up at the start, feathers flapping in readiness for a quick sprint to the finish and maybe a world record, which is currently set at an astonishing three seconds.

Officials sensibly avoid using a starting gun (although that would guarantee some fast times), and on a quieter send-off, the hens are off and ... pecking. Anybody in the crowd expecting a fast sprint soon realises that this is not going to happen. In true wacky style, the hens run around in circles near the start, leaving the crowd in fits of laughter, with the compere egging on the hens as he provides a humorous commentary on the race. Some of the more timid competitors even find their reverse gear and leg it back over the start line towards the nearest bush or car, with their owners in futile pursuit. The rest of the owners remain rooted to the start line and can only shout obscenities at their hens, while their team-mates stand redundantly at the finish line futilely coercing them towards victory.

The races are strictly officiated and Alan Webster, the publican-cum-hen-breeder, adds further humour to the proceedings by handing out yellow cards to the hens for over-indulgent pecking. There is even the possibility of a sending-off for persistent bad behaviour. The hen takes one

look at the red card before stubbornly carrying on running around, requiring the owner to run out on to the track to quell any bitterness among competitors. It must be stressed that the hens are well looked after, with no visible cruelty, apart from perhaps some verbal abuse and 'fowl' language.

Most of the races are particularly slow, and if after five minutes there is still no outcome, the winner is whichever hen is nearest to the finish. Inevitably, one of the competing egg machines will eventually decide to nonchalantly trot over to the finish, oblivious to all the celebratory cheers. Unfortunately, everyone must now wait for the second-place hen to be determined (which enters a consolation race for all the runners-up), and unsurprisingly, there is no third place! The last-placed hen remains ensconced under a bush.

HISTORY

The origins of the event vary depending on who is asked. However, from the organiser himself, the race was set up in 1991 so that he could win something! There are also stories of a rivalry with the neighbouring village of Ible, where hens could have first raced, and there may once have been an egg-laying contest as a precursor to hen racing, but it was Bonsall where the World Championship title was established. The village also lays claim to the last bullfight on English soil and is apparently a Mecca for UFO sightings. Can this place get any weirder?

This is an event rich in amusing stories, including the occasion when, in mid-race, one hen flew off and wasn't found until the next day, despite a mass hen hunt. A past winner won in a matter of seconds, securing the world record in the process, using the underhanded tactic of launching his hen into the air. A new rule has since been introduced requiring hens to keep their feet behind the start line, which has all but ended the chances of the world record ever being broken. During the initial introductions, a family from Yorkshire once proudly admitted how they resorted to pinching a hen on their way to Bonsall so that they could take part ... lucky it wasn't the Wife Carrying Championships!

Finally, the 2007 champion was a hen called Ever Ready, probably a battery hen in a previous life, acquired from the local animal welfare rescue centre. The centre receives money raised from the hen races, and Ever Ready is surely an endorsement for supporting rescue centres elsewhere.

ESSENTIALS

Competitors need to read the list of rules laid out at the start line, which includes no 'fowl' play or laying food on the track. For those without their own hen, or no opportunity to pinch one, the organisers have several feathery beasts available for loan, but make sure you ask upon arrival. Although in 2006, it appeared that the same hen entered into more than one heat, leading to the bizarre conclusion that the hen could be racing herself in the final! Spectators need to keep their dogs on leads, unless, of course, the hens are going too slowly and the restless crowd want to see the race speeded up! The pub serves up delicious food ... including roast chicken (but only those that came last)!

The winning hen receives a bag of grain, with similar prizes for the most attractive hen and the one that ran the straightest, even if it went the wrong way.

TIPS

Train your hen to respond to your voice – this is perhaps why a team of two brothers won the 2005 and 2006 events with their own hen, Wendy. Don't forget to let battery hens stretch their legs before they go hell-for-leather, while free-range competitors will struggle to go anywhere after a lifetime running around in circles.

WACKY FACT

As a prelude to the main races, every year the landlord attempts to break the world record for the fastest 30-foot sprint using his favoured hen, the imaginatively named 'Chicken', in an individual time trial.

IF YOU LIKE THIS

For a slower paced contest, head to Congham in Norfolk for the World Snail Racing Championships (www.snailracing.net) held every July. Over 200 common garden snails race over a distance of thirteen inches on top of a tablecloth. It's hardly motor racing, but the tension mounts as they slither towards the finish line. The current world record is a rapid two minutes, and set by Archie. Fortunately, there is no relay race.

ONION EATING CONTEST

'Don't forget your mouthwash'

Location: Market Square, Newent, Gloucestershire

Date: A Saturday in early September

Time: From midday or 'Cry-Noon'

Entry fee: Free

Further information: Newent Tourist Information, 01531 822468

Grid reference: SO 722 257

Spectator Fun: ★★

Wackiness: ★★

Pain Factor: ★★★

Training Required: ★★

Family Friendly: ★★

WHAT HAPPENS

Among Morris dancers and prized alliums, Newent Onion Fayre also plays host to the annual Onion Eating Contest, where men and women compete to see who can devour an onion in the quickest time ... without bursting into tears!

The men feast on a six-ounce onion, about the size of an apple, while the women are let off with a mere four-ounce onion. Fortunately, none of the entrants are expected to tackle the award-winning, melon-sized beasts on display in the memorial hall!

Women compete first, with challengers less than forth-coming, but with the crowd urging them on, one or two entrants are eventually cajoled into participating. Freshly peeled onions are handed out and the contest begins with collective grimaces from the competitors. Judges are selected from the crowd to ensure none of the competitors attempt to drop any onion rings or add flavour by sneaking a hot dog into the contest!

First bites are large, as entrants tackle the onion in the same way as eating an apple, attempting to complete the bit-ter ordeal as quickly as possible. Beyond the second bite, chewing takes over, and the gurns familiar from other eating contests start to appear as the sharpness hits home and com-petitors find themselves in a bit of a pickle, refusing to turn this into a crying contest. The end of the contest is greeted by a wide open mouth from the winner, while the losers try to hide their joy and relief that the remainder of the onion can be thrown away.

The men's contest is more fiercely competed, with the reigning champion and a former Guinness World Record-

holder lining up on stage alongside experienced onion eaters, absolute novices and the plain hungry, all resembling a row of condemned prisoners, hardly relishing the fate awaiting them. As with the women, the contest begins frantically with big bites all round, but while most of those taking part are content with an average chomp, the reigning champion literally makes his way through half his onion inside fifteen seconds and in the process runs 'onion rings' around his rivals. He is also a fine exponent of the chipmunk technique – even while chewing, further bites are taken so as not to waste time. The rest look on in disbelief at this natural raw talent, while still contending with their first mouthfuls.

The winner is announced around the one-minute mark, and he nonchalantly stands on stage licking his lips, utterly unfazed by the whole proceedings. With no time for handshakes, the other contestants swiftly leave the stage to spit out the unchewed remains.

Both male and female winners receive a trophy for their efforts, but no kisses. Fortunately, there are no second- and third-place prizes, or this contest could well become a test of endurance and end up with half the competitors in hospital with severe indigestion.

HISTORY

Newent Onion Fayre has its origins back in 1105 and received its second charter in 1604. The Onion Eating Contest is less traditional, existing only since 1995. The men's and women's records stand at 1 minute and 1 minute 35 seconds respectively, and both were set in 2007. In recent years the children's category has been cancelled because of insufficient interest ... or should that be too much common sense?

After winning the contest a few years ago, Brian Duffell went on to create a Guinness World Record of 1 minute 30 seconds when he appeared on national television.

ESSENTIALS

The prize onions on display in the community hall are well worth a look, if your stomach and eyes can take it, with the current record a whopping 10 lb. Newent is full of onion stalls, and competitors can seek some relief after the contest by making a dash for the hot dog stands, but don't forget to hold the onions. The high street is closed for cars, but a field on the edge of the town is available for parking.

TIPS

Practice is the obvious advice, while lining the taste buds with milk or beer may lessen the sharp taste slightly. However, as with all eating contests, it's all about minimal chewing and jaw-dropping feats of swallowing ... just don't choke on the onion ring. For the spectators, avoid standing too close to the competitors afterwards ... unless you want to be knocked out. Finally, a tonsorial tip for those who prefer not to take part – the juice from the onion, if spread onto the scalp, is apparently a cure for baldness.

WACKY FACT

The world record, originally held by Brian Duffell, now stands at an eye-watering 48 seconds. Samual Grazette took part in the Barbados Championships and managed the feat in just three bites, attributing his success to a good constitution (and probably plenty of rum).

IF YOU LIKE THIS

You're mad ... but try the World Nettle Eating Championships, held in Marshwood, Dorset, for something even less palatable, where competitors have one hour to eat as many nettle leaves as they can (see page 1).

WORLD BOG SNORKELLING CHAMPIONSHIPS

'You must be flipping mad!'

Location: Waen Rhydd, Llanwrtyd Wells, Powys. Follow the bog signs

Date: August Bank Holiday Monday

Time: From 11am, but arrive early. Prizes awarded late afternoon

Entry fee: £15

Further information: www.green-events.co.uk

Grid reference: SN 882 453

Spectator Fun: ★★★

Wackiness: ★★★★

World Champion: ★★★★

Pain Factor: ★★★

Training Required: ★★★★

Family Friendly: ★★★

WHAT HAPPENS

Competitors actually pay to participate in swimming a race in a cold, pitch-black bog in the middle of a field, in the middle of nowhere, in Wales. With only a snorkel and a pair of flippers required, the person with the fastest time (or should that be least slowest?) becomes World Champion ... The only snag – no recognised swimming stroke is allowed.

In turn, using a mask, snorkel and flippers, entrants must 'swim' to the end of a 60-yard bog before turning around the halfway post and heading back. It's considered de rigueur to wear wetsuits, but there are a few hardy souls who brave the event in trunks only. Bog snorkellers must refrain from raising their head above the water but can pop up briefly should they feel disorientated or develop breathing difficulties. It's definitely advisable to be well acquainted with the art of snorkelling before the event; the bog is not the place to start

learning – unless you intend on literally taking a crash course.

Competitors usually follow convention and kick madly with their flippers, outstretching their arms to remain stream-lined while the hands push any floating debris to the side. Any other unorthodox technique is permitted, even doggy paddle, but this is such a useless stroke in terms of speed that it's far more efficacious to use the recommended method. Then again, if the main aim is to look stupid, then doggy pad-dle could be for you, or maybe a hybrid of crawl and back-stroke. However, any swimming stroke attempted would probably be unrecognisable given the attire and physique of many of the competitors.

Once in the water, there is limited visibility and it's barely possible to pick out the far end. For the most part, eyes focus on the surface of the muddy water swishing around the face, competitors wary of banging into the sides of the extremely narrow bog. Sensibly, the organisers impose a maximum time of two minutes to reach the halfway point, although many will gratefully accept the disqualification.

The return journey becomes increasingly arduous; the legs tire, the snorkel begins to leak in even more fetid water, and the arms feel a desperate urge to attempt some sort of butterfly. It's not uncommon for tired competitors to resem-ble beached whales as they lie stranded halfway back, no energy to kick, their heads and bodies looking like something from a horror film as they briefly emerge to get their bear-ings. With the finish line a mere spot on the horizon – or is that a leech on the mask? – the strugglers begin to feel like they're in a goldfish bowl as the crowd lining both sides of the bog curiously peer down.

The cold water and hostility of the bog may prove too much for a few competitors, but no matter how pathetically they performed, just completing the two lengths is justification enough for a euphoric celebration.

The fastest time, and world record, is 1 minute 35 seconds, set by Joanne Pitchforth in 2007. Ironically, she took the world record off her husband, who could manage only sixth place. For mere mortals, completing the course in less than two minutes is considered a success.

HISTORY

Conceived by Gordon Green (founder of Green Events) back in 1985 to raise money for the local town, it has since got bigger and bigger and has even seen a second bog created to accommodate more idiots. For some entrants, fast times are the last thing on their mind, preferring to display a comical approach to the race. One year, a man dressed in an inflatable sumo costume barely managed to fit inside the bog. Once in, he resembled a floating pig ... the sympathetic officials, however, allowed him to finish the course in his own time!

There was even more amusement when two brave entrants decided to double their humiliation and contest the event in drag costumes, requiring frequent breaks along the way to empty water from their handbags and adjust their dresses. Spectators are not excluded from the humiliation – one year, a cameraman became too excited cheering on a competitor and fell into the bog himself!

ESSENTIALS

Flippers and snorkel are compulsory for the swim. However, mono fins and scuba gear are definitely not permitted, and while the bog isn't too cold, wetsuits are advisable if you have an aversion to any creepy crawlies, particularly eels, leeches and water scorpions!

A fast start is always helpful, but on no account attempt to dive into the bog, which is only a couple of feet deep, as one competitor found out the hard way in 2006, when his over-eagerness to make a splash ended with a nose bleed.

Minimum age to take part is fourteen years, with no maximum; one year, even a 70-year-old woman competed. Junior participants are permitted to rest halfway with the clock paused. There is a clean stream nearby for those who would rather not drive home covered in mud and looking like the bogman.

This is a difficult event to find. Follow the bog signs as you enter the town. As you approach Llanwrtyd Wells from Llandovery, take the road right, past Dolwen Fields, and follow for one mile. Then follow the track to the right, which will take you into the car park. Alternatively, just follow the odd-looking people in wetsuits and flippers walking by the roadside!

WACKY FACT

Due to a severe shortage of water drying up the bog in 1995, the contest had to be cancelled; maybe they should have renamed the event the bog crawl! The event also failed to take place in 2001 because of foot and mouth disease ... but that would be the least of the bog snorkellers' worries.

TIPS

Strong leg action is essential. A former record holder was an international swimmer, so plenty of reps in the local pool beforehand will help – throw in a few sheep and some weeds to recreate the full sensuous experience. A good pair of well-fitting flippers is vital, otherwise, if one comes off, as a competitor discovered in 2006, you will find it almost impossible to make any headway.

If you are intent on winning, ensure you have an early start. As the day progresses, reeds, lost competitors and disturbed mud will clog the bog up, hindering both movement and visibility. Finally, don't forget to save plenty of energy for the return leg; the bog deludes most entrants into thinking how short it looks.

IF YOU LIKE THIS

Northern Ireland have their own Bog Snorkelling Championships, but if that's not enough of a challenge, the organisers in Llanwrtyd Wells also offer the Bog Snorkelling Triathlon, involving a twelve-mile run, a 25-mile cycle and, of course, two lengths of bog snorkelling. The fastest time is two hours 30 minutes, and competitors face the added dilemma of overtaking in the bog. It's only a matter of time before Gordon Green conceives the quadrathlon, requiring competitors to canoe up and down the bog!

OLNEY PANCAKE RACE

'A quick flip and they're off'

Location: High Street, Olney, near Milton Keynes, Buckinghamshire

Date: Shrove Tuesday

Time: 11.55am

Entry fee: Free

Further information: www.olneytowncouncil.co.uk/pancake.php

Grid reference: SP 889 153

Spectator Fun: ★★

Wackiness: ★★★

Family Friendly: ★★★

WHAT HAPPENS

After a morning indulging in copious pancakes, around fifteen local women line up outside the Bull Hotel in Olney, dressed in traditional 1950s housewife attire of apron, headscarf and stockings. Clutching their frying pans with a pancake that they have personally cooked, they are set for a fast dash to church. Unfortunately, house-husbands are not allowed to enter.

At 11.55am, the church warden starts the race by asking competitors, 'Toss your pancakes, are you ready?' He then rings the pancake bell which is normally kept in the town museum. After a flip of the pancake, everyone sets off through the town towards the parish church where the finish is, 415 yards later. The race is very often two-tiered, with the 'fun' entrants at the back. One year, two people decided to run the course three-legged. Maybe the spare leg tossed the pancakes!

Competitors need to have plenty of coordination as they manoeuvre around the tight bends and occasional human obstacles while balancing the frying pan to avert any accidental tossing. Losing the pancake is the main concern, and many competitors cook an unusually thick pancake that could easily be mistaken for a pizza, which is unlikely to slip around, while also firmly holding it down with their thumb. Runners are expected to flip the pancake at least once during their run.

The winning time is around 70 seconds, with the majority of runners some way behind – having probably eaten too many pancakes beforehand. The winner must nervously toss her pancake once again at the end, before receiving kisses

from the vicar and verger – is that why competitors take their time? Everyone then heads into church for the Shriving service, with frying pans placed around the font and plenty of sweating, panting housewives on the front pews.

HISTORY

One of the oldest wacky events, with the first race believed to have been run as early as 1445, and so ingrained into local culture that even the town's welcome sign features the pancake racers. There are two possible explanations as to why the race started. Many believe it all began after a housewife heard the church's Shriving bells while she was making pancakes and promptly ran to church, with frying pan in hand. However, it's debatable whether there were frying pans back in the 15th century. Pancakes were also thought to be a bribe to the bell ringer, to bring forward the Shriving service which acts as a prelude to a period of festivity. The race took place even during the tumultuous Wars of the Roses, and today's race has been run continually since 1948.

In 1950, the American town of Liberal, Kansas saw photographs of the pancake race and challenged the town of Olney to a dual pancake race, each one held over the same distance, although in Liberal the competitors run with skillets, not frying pans. To make conditions fair, Liberal even designed their course on a four-lane highway, including every bend and nuance that runners in Olney follow.

Every year the two towns exchange dignitaries and the overall winner is declared following a tense phone call at 6.30pm, allowing both races to finish and a trophy to be awarded to whichever race winner had the fastest time.

The race has been declared void only once, back in 1980, when Liberal had its own interruption, with a BBC television crew inadvertently blocking the course. Liberal also make the day more action-packed, and in the true American way they organise an all-you-can-eat pancake breakfast and a pancake eating contest. Presumably, these two events end up becoming entwined into one mass meal. It's a wonder that more people from Olney don't jet off to the other side of the Atlantic.

ESSENTIALS

There are strict rules on who can take part in the race. Only women over eighteen years old are eligible and they must have their permanent home in Olney, or have resided in the town for at least three months prior to Shrove Tuesday. While it has been traditional for housewives to take part, unmarried women can also enter ... as long as they know how to cook pancakes. Besides the overall winner, there are further prizes awarded to the oldest competitor and to the last person home. Should one of the competitors take long enough, they could win both these prizes!

The festivities begin at 10am with a children's race, run along a much shorter course, and after the main race all visitors are invited to the Shriving service. Later in the evening there is the pancake race party, and throughout the day a total of 800 pancakes are cooked.

The race itself is over very quickly and unless you can outsprint the winner you will be unable to see both the start and finish – so find a good vantage point along the course. There is also a pretend start by the competitors for the benefit of all the photographers.

TIPS

If you are not a local, moving to Olney for three months prior to the race will guarantee you an entry. If you're a man, shaving your legs and wearing drag may be enough to convince the judges, but you will still need to be able to toss a pancake ... twice! For those eligible to take part, without bending the rules, it helps to be fit enough to run the 415 yards and still have enough energy to flip the pancake and kiss the vicar. A lightweight pan may save a few seconds in the race, while taking a frying pan out on your training runs will improve coordination.

---(**WACKY FACT**)---

In 1948, the local vicar discovered old photographs of the race and managed to persuade thirteen volunteers to recreate the race, which has carried on ever since.

---(**IF YOU LIKE THIS**)---

There are many pancake races held throughout the country on Shrove Tuesday, including contests at Lichfield, Bradford-on-Avon (which also incorporates a men's race) and High Wycombe, where teams of local businesses take part. The Old Truman Brewery in Brick Lane, London stages the Great Spitalfields Pancake Race, where teams of four compete for the prize of an engraved frying pan.

But Wimborne Minster in Dorset is the place to be for non-stop pancake tossing action. For a whole hour, toddlers, children, adults and even wheelchair-bound pensioners compete in a series of exciting races (not all at once, thankfully!), around the Minster. If the tight corners were not enough of a challenge, competitors must also toss their pancake at four points along the short course. With over twenty races (plus some relays), this is one place where there will definitely be no sweet food left over for Lent.

WORLD CLOG COBBING CHAMPIONSHIPS

'A throwing contest with a watery twist'

Location:	Roebuck Inn, 482 Burnley Road, Rawtenstall, Lancashire
Date:	Easter Monday
Time:	Starts at 1pm and continues all afternoon
Entry fee:	£1 for three throws
Further information:	Roebuck Inn, 01706 214174
Grid reference:	SD 836 232

Spectator Fun:	★★
Wackiness:	★★★
World Champion:	★★★
Pain Factor:	★
Training Required:	★★
Family Friendly:	★★★

WHAT HAPPENS

When it comes to conceiving a throwing event, it's certainly a case of it being 'queer up north', as competitors 'cobb a clog' – or chuck an old working boot, for those unfamiliar with northern dialect.

Competitors attempt to throw the clog as far as possible down a back street, next to the Roebuck Inn. This is no straightforward throwing contest, as the clog must be hurled backwards over the shoulder and, more importantly, avoid landing in the river, which is tantalisingly close. If throwing normally isn't your forte, then this could be an event for you.

Choosing from a selection of well-worn but not too smelly clogs, competitors take turns to have three throws. Besides facing away from the direction of the cobb, there are additional unorthodox rules for throwers to remember, including

gripping the clog with both hands and electing to take hold of the heel, toe or tongue only – but then, where else could you grip?

There is a standard throw used by all competitors, although even this single technique has variations within it. Typically, the thrower grabs hold of the clog tightly and then crouches down with knees bent and backside sticking out. After a final check of their bearings and making sure they are not aiming straight for the river, they begin to swing the clog back and forth through the legs – this is therefore not an event to enter in tight jeans or a short skirt!

For serious contenders, the swinging is the key to success, and after about five or six swings they will loft the clog over their head, accompanied by a loud roar or sometimes an aggressive squeak! The thrower then takes a nervous glance forward, hoping the clog will fly a considerable distance down the road, avoiding the tree, the river and the woman standing innocently with the measuring tape. The less enthusiastic entrants are more blasé about the whole thing and nonchalantly hurl the clog but still manage to post a creditable distance.

For a throw to count, the clog must land on the road. The distance is then measured from where it hits the ground, and not where it finally rolls to a standstill. A few years ago this rule was at the centre of a very heated debate. Officials scrutinised the official Clog Cobbing Association rulebook (probably written on the back of a beer mat) to discount a potentially winning throw after the clog bounced along the ground several times.

Accuracy is therefore essential, but to add further woes there is a 50p penalty for any throw accidentally finding the river. Entrants may even be volunteered to retrieve the clog themselves via a ladder should they repeat the feat a second time. Possible candidates for wayward throws should be aware that negotiating the ladder is a challenge in itself. It's not known what penalty the officials bestow on anyone unlucky enough to throw the clog in the river for a third time, but last place is probably punishment enough.

Competitors should also pay attention to a large tree to the left of the road, providing another tricky obstacle to avoid. If the river doesn't get the clog, maybe the branches will. Fortunately, though, competitors are not required to climb trees to retrieve their clogs.

Anything over 40 feet is deemed respectable, while the winning man and woman usually throw in excess of 90 feet and 60 feet respectively.

HISTORY

No one is certain of the exact origins, with many mixed opinions to when, where and how the event started. There was definitely an event back in the 1970s, although rumour has it that another pub, the Buck Inn in nearby Cowpe, first conceived the event. There is even talk that a black pudding was thrown instead.

Further confusion concerns the world record, with one man believed to have hurled the clog a whopping 280 feet; but with the usual efforts achieving no more than 100 feet, this is probably a gross over-estimate embellished over time. Who knows, in ten years' time the record may have increased to 400 feet!

The event has also attracted its fair share of humour, with a misdirected clog somehow flying forwards, not backwards, and smashing a window belonging to the pub across the road. Another time, one unfortunate spectator had his nose broken when a hurled clog headed the wrong way into the crowd. Spectators should therefore not stand too close to the throwers, lest the clog flies off on an unexpected trajectory. However, judging from some of the throws witnessed, the only safe person is the actual thrower.

ESSENTIALS

There are food and drink prizes for men, ladies, lads and lasses, with plenty of alcoholic drink in close proximity. Besides the Clog Cobbing, there are various charity stalls to keep children occupied and even a tug-of-war competition, once all the clogs have been lost in the river.

TIPS

Seasoned competitors advise developing a good swing and a firm grip, usually holding on to the heel of the clog, but brute strength will always gain a few extra feet. Competitors arriving early may have the opportunity for a few practice throws. A straight throw overhead is also crucial to avoid the 50p fine and the possibility of an impromptu bathe in the river.

IF YOU LIKE THIS

There is the World Black Pudding Throwing Championships in nearby Ramsbottom (see page 289), but for more smelly footwear try a 'Welly Wanging' contest. One of the better known competitions takes place at the National Wetland Centre, near Llanelli, South Wales. The contest involves chucking a wellington boot across a river estuary and is one of several mud-themed activities at the National Mud Festival every September. For further information, go to www.wwt.org.uk.

WORLD GURNING CHAMPIONSHIP

'A beauty contest with an ugly twist'

Location:	Market Hall, Egremont, Cumbria
Date:	Third Saturday in September
Time:	From 6pm till late
Entry fee:	Free
Further information:	www.egremontcrabfair.org.uk
Grid reference:	NY 010 108

Spectator Fun:	★
Wackiness:	★★
World Champion:	★★
Pain Factor:	★
Training Required:	★★★
Family Friendly:	★★

WHAT HAPPENS

The flip side to Miss World, where contestants have the vain hope of becoming the World Gurning Champion. Gurning is all about transforming the face to produce monstrous and downright horrific expressions. Unfortunately, those who are naturally ugly need not apply to enter. Eerily, the event takes place down the road from Sellafield nuclear power station, perhaps giving the locals an unfair advantage over outsiders.

Gurning is the final event to take place on a day of bizarre contests, and after four hours of copious drinking and furtive face pulling in the bathroom mirror, gurners finally take their turn in the limelight. Arriving on stage, contestants face immediate indignity by placing their head through a braffin, or horse's collar. Then, to the accompaniment of such ironically titled music as 'You're Gorgeous' and 'I'm Your Man',

they begin to twist and contort their faces into grotesque, gorgon-like expressions. They turn to the panel of judges first, before being paraded to the crowd, while hoping that the wind doesn't change during their gurn!

Unsurprisingly, the majority of entrants barely manage a childlike grimace, instead creating the impression that they are in the throes of diarrhoea, or perhaps choking on a peanut. A quick exhalation of air, blowing out of the cheeks and going cross-eyed is the best they can manage, although one or two entrants are able to rotate their eyes in opposite directions, inadvertently adding comedy to the evening. The more experienced gurners come back year after year, and their attempts appear genuinely gruesome as they revel in their talents. Many have dedicated their life to working on their face, trying out various combinations until they discover a winning formula.

The current World Champion, Tommy Mattinson, is the final contestant of the evening, entering the room to a cacophony of cheering, clapping and foot stamping. After a tense pause, Tommy slowly moves his hands away from his face to reveal a truly horrific look, as he snarls at the crowd. His transformation into the Incredible Hulk is complete. Tommy has made a living from his gurns, and victory is a foregone conclusion as he parades on stage like a prized caged animal, offering several encores until his facial muscles cramp up. Kisses from the judges are not forthcoming, however. Just how does someone know they have such a talent in the first place?

HISTORY

There are several possible origins of gurning – one theory goes back to the 13th century, when a farmhand bit into a crab apple and pulled a funny face. Other stories recall a village idiot being mocked and a farmer berating his wife for looking ugly. Whatever the reason, face pulling contests have become a popular form of entertainment at fairs around the world, and since the 1970s the World Championship has even included a contest for women and children … which was not long after the nuclear power station was built!

It has certainly been a case of 'gurning in the family' for the Mattinsons. Gordon Mattinson and his son Tommy have both won the event several times. This begs the question of whether they spent their evenings practising at the dinner table, trying to out-gurn each other.

Marie Quinn, a former USA champion, has the distinction of becoming the only female competitor to finish in the top three when she entered in 1974. The youngest-ever contestant was a baby whose gurn was created by its mother putting a lemon into its mouth to suck on. On another occasion the judges declared the wrong winner, causing uproar, with bottles thrown on the stage in protest.

ESSENTIALS

The championship is the highlight of Egremont Crab Fair, established in 1267, and takes place alongside a greasy pole contest and horn blowing. The winner of the Gurning receives a prize of £100 and, like previous champions, attains minor celebrity status, appearing in commercials and television chat shows. The licensed venue is quite small, so arrive early to guarantee a seat. The contest does not usually finish until 11pm, but could go on much later should the results not please the crowd.

TIPS TO WIN

The transformation in the face is crucial to winning, which means that natural ugliness is not necessarily a pre-requisite for victory – in fact it may be a hindrance. Competitors are encouraged to jump around and grunt noisily to improve their chances. One former entrant even removed all his remaining teeth to enhance his looks, but we don't recommend such drastic action for a one-off performance.

Regular practice before the event was the advice of the current reigning World Champion – just make sure the mirror you intend to crack isn't too valuable. Past champions have drawn inspiration from watching old horror movies, even giving pet names to their gurns, such as the 'Werewolf' or 'Quasimodo'.

WACKY FACT

The 2006 women's champion, Anne Woods, is also an Avon lady – obviously she could do with a few more free samples herself.

IF YOU LIKE THIS

If your looks failed to make an impact at the Gurning contest, head to Miss World or Crufts to garner some tips, but don't expect to win either of these contests, no matter how hard you try. There is also the World Beard and Moustache Championships for those who prefer to cover up their good looks. The global contest is staged biennially and in 2007 the event came to Brighton, where hirsute entrants proudly displayed their Dalis, Garibaldis and freestyle sideburns.

THE GREAT SHIRT RACE

*'A rare opportunity to drink and drive
without being pulled over'*

Location: Bampton, Oxfordshire

Date: Spring Bank Holiday Saturday

Time: From 5pm

Entry fee: None

Further information:
www.bamptonoxon.co.uk/
annual_events.htm

Grid reference: SP 314 032

Spectator Fun: ★★

Wackiness: ★

Pain Factor: ★

Training Required: ★

Family Friendly: ★★★

WHAT HAPPENS

A race organised by the SPAJERS, and contested by tequila-laden mules and dining tables ... how daft can it get?

Not a contest for blouses and polo necks as the name suggests, but a pub crawl with a difference which sees human-powered vehicles race through the village of Bampton. The rules are very simple: the vehicle must have wheels and be self-propelled, with one person pushing and a second team member pulling, if necessary. The third member of the team has the easier task (when sober) of sitting within the contraption.

Dependent on whether they have the winning post in mind or prefer to earn laughs from the crowd, enjoying their drinks as they go, the rest of the entertainment is up to the ingenuity and imagination of the teams.

After a mass start, teams dash to the first drink stop, avoiding local children armed with water bombs who are seeking an opportunity to soak everyone.

The course then follows existing and former public houses as it winds its way through the village. When the race first started over 40 years ago there were about eleven pubs, which probably resulted in many headaches for those taking part. Only four pubs remain today, with the drink stations located outside for teams to drink their beer: one pint for the blokes and half a pint for the ladies. Officials are on hand to ensure that there are no time-saving spillages from the more devious teams.

Residents of the former pubs often provide an alfresco bar on their doorstep to make up the shortage, ensuring that no one finishes too quickly or soberly. After each pit stop, team members must swap over duties – that is, if they can coordinate themselves without falling over.

The quicker teams hurtle around the course getting hot under the collar as they jostle for pole position, while avoiding any potential collisions. The winning teams usually race with streamlined wheelbarrows, prams or wheelie bins and finish in ten minutes, hardly enough time for the beer to go down. Slower entrants, meanwhile, narrowly avoid slipping over on puddles of beer left behind by their speedier colleagues as they meander along.

The course contains several tricky bends for the teams to negotiate. One unusual entry which arrived as a dining table, complete with food and candelabra, found the route particularly challenging as the team pushed themselves around the course. The table was almost the width of the road, and the team even ate a banquet meal as they went along.

For most teams, though, it's all about the fancy dress and drinking as they crawl around the course, becoming steadily more intoxicated and losing control of their vehicle. In fact, any semblance of a formation to the team has long since disappeared, and it's a free-for-all on who steers, pushes and staggers! Amusing past entries have included a fire engine (with real firemen), a cowboy wagon and a motorbike disguised as a tank, but it was the team that dressed as the 'Three Amigos' who produced the biggest laughs. Wearing Mexican ponchos and sporting ridiculous moustaches, they attempted to push round a mule on wheels, which had a mind of its own.

No fast times were expected from the Three Amigos, who not only took their time at each drink stop, but even added some additional stops into the route, lifting the mule's rear end to reveal bottles of tequila. Top marks for invention, but unfortunately at the final drink station they had become so inebriated that they dropped an unopened bottle in the middle of the street.

HISTORY

The Shirt Race started in 1953, as a celebration of the coronation. John Quick and Paul Bovington, of the Society for the Preservation of Ancient Junketing (SPAJERS), came up with the idea to raise money for the local hospital. It now funds an annual coach trip for the pensioners in the village.

Originally, teams dressed in Wee Willie Winkie nightshirts, hence the name, and used prams to get around. As fashion trends changed, though, a shortage of nightgowns was almost the downfall of the race. Fortunately, it was agreed that alternative fancy dress could be allowed, thereby guaranteeing that the race went ahead and setting a precedent for future contests.

There is one very good reason why the drink stations are outside the public houses. One team a few years ago decided that, having drunk their quota, they would stay for an extra pint or two ... and then another one after that! Eventually the team returned to the race, managing to complete the course only five minutes before closing time.

ESSENTIALS

Best vantage points for those not taking part are towards the end of the course, when competitors are beginning to feel the effects of the beer and find their coordination and steering wayward. Spectators beware ... there are several water bomb fights throughout the evening aimed at the competing teams, but as children are not always careful where they throw things, don't forget to take your umbrella, and don't park your car on the main street!

There are also shorter races for juniors, with older children running the same course as the adults, but drinking orange juice instead of beer, which leaves no excuse for bad driving. The prize for the fastest team and best fancy dress involves beer or food.

---(TIPS)---

To win, teams will need to be fit, be able to drink beer swiftly (without a bib) and have a lightweight entry that will get them around the course quickly. For most of the teams taking part, though, the only flawless part of the race will be the drinking.

---(WACKY FACT)---

With the Shirt Race in full flow one year, Prince Charles arrived in Bampton to hear some chamber music in the local church, oblivious of the more exciting tradition taking place out on the street.

IF YOU LIKE THIS

This is just one of many charity races involving beer and flamboyantly decorated wheelbarrows or wheelie bins. Two more well-known events are the Three Horseshoes Wheelie Bin Race, held in Staplestreet, Kent (see page 225) and the Gambo Race in Kenfig, near Bridgend, South Wales, held every August. Home-made carts tackle a short course that incorporates around eight pubs and, not surprisingly, the 'race' takes all day to complete.

EXMOUTH CHRISTMAS DAY DIP

'Don't forget the duck fat!'

Location:	The Clock Tower, Exmouth sea front, Devon
Date:	Christmas Day
Time:	11am
Entry fee:	Free
Further information:	Exmouth Tourist Information, 01395 222299
Grid reference:	SY 001 804

Spectator Fun:	★★
Wackiness:	★★
Pain Factor:	★★★★
Training Required:	★
Family Friendly:	★★★★

WHAT HAPPENS

The festive season is not all about presents and day-long eating contests. Hundreds of people will amble out of bed with a hangover to head for a Christmas Day sea swim, where stupidity and stamina are the main requirements for participation, and the only thing peeled will be your clothes.

For many, even in summertime, the sea is hardly inviting, and at the end of the year the allure of the sea fades completely as the water cools to a very chilly three degrees. With an even cooler air temperature and Siberian winds adding to the grim experience, the prospect of a quick swim on Christmas Day loses its appeal. But this doesn't stop up to 300 mad and crazy locals descending on Exmouth beach for an unseasonal dip in an array of fancy dress, usually Santa Claus outfits, with some fancily undressed. Spectators, who line the promenade, are sensibly fully clothed in full winter regalia

and succeed in making the swimmers feel even colder as they head for the beach.

With minutes to go, swimmers jettison jumpers and bin liners, and psych themselves up while rubbing their bodies to keep the goose bumps away. Before the big off, all competitors turn to face the crowd for a pathetically sung chorus of 'We wish you a Merry Christmas', drowned out by the sound of chattering teeth. The crowd reciprocate with a more uplifting version. The Mayor, who wisely decides not to partake in the dip himself, finally gives the sign and there is a dramatic dash towards the sea.

The foolhardy ones who race to be the first in are usually the first to squeal as the cold water laps around their bare flesh, while others hold hands in trepidation as they hit the surf, wrongly assuming that entering the water together will relieve some of the discomfort. Wading in slowly and easing themselves into deeper and deeper water, they finally dive in, unwilling to prolong their fate, and frantically swim in a vain attempt to get warm.

The swim is as brief as the costumes on display, with nearly everyone attempting only a couple of strokes, perhaps instead taking part in the Christmas Day 'Drip', before retreating towards the sanctuary of a warm beach towel.

A small minority, after overcoming the initial shock and taken over by a numbness from head to toe, will admirably strive for a more meaningful swim until their extremities begin turning a worrying shade of blue. Others stubbornly strive to be the last one out. Eventually, the lifeguards clear the water and the stragglers finally make a very quick exit to thaw out with a hot toddy.

HISTORY

The first dip took place in the 1960s with a few friends (only because the indoor pool was closed) and has slowly gained momentum since then. The organiser initially kept a register of all participants, including a Canadian entrant in 1981, but in the last ten years this has become a practical nightmare as numbers have risen and often people decide to join or exit the dip at the very last minute.

In 2006, a grandmother overcame her fear of water, which had begun when she slipped head-first into a swimming pool as a child, by participating in the swim. In the process she raised £1,000 for charity, but vowed that once was enough. Dippers have ranged from six months to 98 years old, although neither record-holder was probably in the sea for long.

ESSENTIALS

Rules are simple: no wetsuits allowed and have fun. There is no official charity (sadly, due to insurance costs), but individuals are encouraged to raise money themselves. The RNLI and beach lifeguards are present should anyone find themselves besieged with cramp, but on no account should anyone swim out to the lifeboat.

The sea is a big step up from the local indoor pool. If the Christmas Dip is a one-off, enter the water gradually to avert any risk of a heart attack and be careful leaving the sea if there is a large swell. It's not a rare sight for swimmers to exit the sea without their trunks or bikini after wrestling with a large wave. After the swim, many head off to the pub next to the beach.

TIPS

For the majority, the swim will be a quick plunge in and out, but for anything more, it's advisable to keep warm beforehand and avoid too much bravado. Dippers usually gather on the beach 30 minutes before the start, so wear clothes you can quickly discard. A layer of Vaseline around more sensitive areas of the body will relieve some of the shock while not betraying your concession to some comfort. Wearing a swim cap will keep in some of the warmth, even though you will look like an oversized condom as you troop into the water.

For serious training, the sea is at its warmest in September – a tropical sixteen degrees – and this is therefore the optimum time to begin sea swimming, allowing the body enough time to acclimatise. Should a panic attack come on while in the water, it's recommended that you float on your back, close your eyes and simply kick your legs with your head pointed towards the shoreline. Most importantly, ensure that warm clothing and a hot drink are available immediately afterwards, ideally followed by a ready cooked Christmas meal.

IF YOU LIKE THIS

The Serpentine Lake in Hyde Park, London also stages an annual Christmas Day swim, the Peter Pan Cup, which sees swimmers racing 100 yards. The race is run on a handicap system and has been staged since 1904, and is so called after the Peter Pan originator, James Barrie, who presented the first trophy. Unfortunately, swimmers need to be club members who have entered races throughout the previous year to earn the right to take part. The Christmas Day swim starts at 9am, and unlike the sea swims there is no hanging around, with everyone diving or jumping straight in, off the pontoon.

There are many other established sea and lake swims throughout the festive season, up and down the British coastline from Brighton to Sunderland to Jersey. Budleigh Salterton, next door to Exmouth, also holds a Christmas Day swim at the earlier time of 10am, allowing the truly insane to partake in two sea swims! On Boxing Day, there is the Albert Dock Dip in Liverpool and the Walrus Dip at Pembrey Country Park, Carmarthenshire, where in previous years swimmers have been consoled with a small whisky. Other well known swims include the New Year's Day Dip at Peel, Isle of Man and the Loony Dook in South Queensferry, near Edinburgh. The website, www.outdoorswimmingsociety.com, has a full list of festive dips, plus an exhaustive list of recommended spots in rivers, lakes and seas for swimming during the rest of the year.

WORLD CONKER CHAMPIONSHIPS

'Who will be the conqueror?'

Location:	Ashton, near Oundle, Northamptonshire
Date:	Second Sunday in October
Time:	Registration before 10am. Contest begins from 10.30am
Entry fee:	£10 in advance

Further information:
www.worldconkerchampionships.com

Grid reference:	TL 055 883

Spectator Fun:	★★
Wackiness:	★★
World Champion:	★★★
Pain Factor:	★
Training Required:	★★★
Family Friendly:	★★★★

WHAT HAPPENS

It's back to school for the classic game of conkers. The event is a knockout tournament for men, ladies and juniors with a very international feel: 500 contestants from nineteen countries, including Brazil and India, a samba band, and even an Olympic-style flag-waving parade as a prelude to the championships.

In an arena of eight conker 'pitches', players are split into six pools, four male and two female. Play commences with competitors choosing their conker, already drilled and laced by the organisers. Unfortunately, competitors are not permitted to bring their prized 'twenty-fiver' conker, which they fought with back in their school days. It also means no home-made conkers baked in an oven with vinegar, soaked in paraffin or coated in nail varnish, but maybe they will introduce a

specialist category in future to cater for the more entrepreneurial or devious competitor?

A toss of the coin determines the order of play, with the first striker gaining the massive advantage, since it takes only one solid shot on target to win. This also means a competitor can lose and go home without a swing of the conker. The players square up on a raised platform and the striker requests the height at which their opponent must hold the conker, which can involve much pedantic adjustment, before proceeding to take three shots. After each shot both competitors stare towards the end of the string, to see whether the conker is still clinging on, followed by sighs of relief or frustration. Strikes are then exchanged until one of the conkers is deemed unfit for further combat, usually decided by the sight of the conker flying into the crowd or shattering all over the arena. To remain in the contest a conker must be 'enough to mount an attack', and it could be a test of sheer

stubbornness as competitors do battle with nothing more than the relics of the shell.

Each match is well officiated to ensure the rules are observed, including holding the lace at a set distance of 20cm between the knuckle and the nut, and elimination if you 'snag' your opponent's lace three times in a match. The referee even has a ruler at hand, ready to dive in and argue over a few millimetres. The stamps rule (where a conker knocked from an opponent's hand on to the floor can be crushed if the striker shouts stamp first) that was enthusiastically played in the school playground is fortunately not allowed. Instead, any conker knocked off the lace intact can be re-threaded. Finally, there is the five-minute rule, where if neither conker has been smashed after this time, each player has nine more shots, taken alternately. If both the conkers remain intact, the player who made the most contacts from their nine strikes will win.

Fresh conkers are provided every round, although it would probably be more fun for the crowd to see players do battle with pieces of lace! As the contest reaches the final stages, the tension mounts as strikes become more accurate and powerful. While luck plays its part, skill and experience will always see the better players progress. The overall winners are crowned King and Queen Conker, and have the honour of sitting down on specially made thrones.

HISTORY

The pastime of conkers may have originally derived from a game played in France, where they used snail shells (the

French for conch is *conque*) instead of horse chestnuts. The French version involved placing the shell in a fist, hopefully without the snail still residing inside, and their opponent would squeeze the hand until it broke. The Isle of Wight lays claim to the first recorded game of conkers with horse chestnuts in Britain, back in 1848. The island now hosts the British Junior Championships.

The inaugural World Championship was organised by locals as an alternative to a fishing weekend when bad weather prevailed. Around 300 men and over 100 women enter the contest each year, and since its conception back in 1965 a staggering £250,000 has been raised for charity.

The contest has had its close shaves. Organisers in 2003 had to request conkers from elsewhere after 'global warming' caused conkers in Northamptonshire to fall prematurely. The following year a Cumbrian teacher's safety campaign to stop children playing conkers very nearly precipitated the event's demise. Consequently, all competitors that same year were required to wear safety goggles. In 2007, the Institute of Health and Safety showed a more light-hearted side when they decided to sponsor the contest, even entering a team themselves – no sign of any hard hats or safety vests anywhere! There is also the looming presence of the leaf miner moth, or *Cameraria ohridella*, and a disease called bleeding canker, which threaten to ruin future conker harvests.

ESSENTIALS

Advance registration is essential to guarantee entry (usually before June, but no later than 1 October). There is also a

small charge for spectators (£4 adults and £2 children/senior citizens). This is one event where fancy dress will attract attention, and in past years competitors have arrived as bananas, pirates and nuns and gone home completely nuts.

There is also a team event, where the scores in the individual competition are added together. Children can take part, entering on the day and playing the earlier rounds in a smaller arena away from the adult contest, but the more successful junior entrants are given a chance to display their conquering credentials in the main arena for the last few rounds.

(TIPS)

The organisers have done everything possible to minimise cheating, but this has not precluded some competitors in the past trying to smuggle in painted stones disguised as conkers. Underhanded tactics are definitely not encouraged and eagle-eyed referees will spot any foul play. The sure-fire way to success is plenty of practice and a good aim – the 2006 champion admitted practising every night for six months leading up to the contest.

But for the majority who haven't played conkers since they were in short trousers, there are a few tactics to try, as described by conkers expert, John Hadman: 'There are various stances or swings. Some people favour the over-arm swing, where the conker comes down vertically. Others go in from the side or diagonally, reckoning that it's perhaps easier to go against the softer part of the nut – and then there is the side-slash, the forward side-slash, and the backhand side-slash.'

Then it's all down to luck: whether the conker allocated will be stronger and harder than your opponent's.

A less well-known tip is to scrutinise your conker prior to combat. Every official conker is holed with an electric drill and, depending on the craftsmanship of the driller, the conker may be left with nasty cracks susceptible to a powerful strike. Competitors can therefore replace their chosen conker and select another.

WACKY FACT NO. 1

A former World Champion admitted that the best way to harden the conker for combat was by passing it through the stomach of a pig and then finding it some time later!

WACKY FACT NO. 2

There is a second way to fight with conkers. During the First World War, horse chestnuts were in demand because of their starch content, which was an important ingredient for making ammunition. Just don't tell any bad losers at the contest … they may be inspired to go to extreme lengths to prove a point!

IF YOU LIKE THIS

The Vale of Belvoir Conker Championships, at the Crown and Plough in Long Clawson, Leicestershire, takes place a week before the World Championships, offering beginners some competitive practice and an introduction to conker etiquette.

THE GREAT KNARESBOROUGH BED RACE

'Make sure your bed slippers are waterproof'

Location:	Knaresborough, West Yorkshire
Date:	Saturday in mid-June
Time:	Parade from 1pm. Race starts 3pm
Entry fee:	£60 per team

Further information:
www.knaresborough.co.uk/bedrace

Grid reference:	SE 342 573

Spectator Fun:	★★
Wackiness:	★★★
Pain Factor:	★★★★
Training Required:	★★★★
Family Friendly:	★★★

WHAT HAPPENS

There is no need to get out of bed for this mad race around Knaresborough, with teams racing along a short, hilly and very wet course with makeshift beds.

The race begins and ends at Conyngham Hall, passing several local public houses. But there's no time for the teams to stop for a swift pint. Instead, competitors have the opportunity to taste the local river water towards the end of the race!

Each team consists of six runners, a bed, and one 'bedridden' passenger, who must be of the opposite sex. There is a staggered start to prevent mass carnage, with the fastest teams setting off first and those entering the race for laughs starting last. The lightweight, aerodynamic build of the quicker beds will be easier to pick out from the rest, where fancy dress takes precedence over performance.

The first part of the three-kilometre course is gentle, following the River Nidd and allowing the teams to bed themselves in. Then, about halfway along, is the first of the two notoriously difficult sections with a very steep climb to the Castle Top, a gradient of 1 in 5. This is the point when the fitter teams prosper. For the rest, it will be a matter of simply getting to the top without letting go of the bed, with the passenger keeping their eyes firmly shut and gripping on to the side until the bed has reached the safety of the summit.

The course then bends back towards the start, even including a fast downhill section, affording the teams much-needed respite before they reach the point in the race that everyone dreads, but spectators look forward to – the river crossing.

Entry into the river is the trickiest part, and teams must tilt the bed almost vertically before plunging down into the water, praying it remains upright and afloat. If disaster is to strike, it will happen here. Despite the 30-second intervals at the start line, beds will inevitably congest when they reach the river, and often more than one team is in the river at the same time. Frogmen are on hand should there be any 'Titanic' struggles, and every year there are always a few capsizes.

Once afloat, competitors will nervously doggy paddle alongside the bed towards the opposite bank, battling against the flow of the river. An error-free climb back on to dry land leaves a short sprint to the finish line. The fastest teams usually complete the course in less than fifteen minutes. It's not surprising that the local running club often finish in the quickest time.

Back at the start, the slower, more entertaining teams are setting off – completing the course safely is their only ambition. Teams find out early on in the race whether they have compromised the mechanics for too much decoration, and one or two entries often spectacularly collapse within yards of the start line, sadly having to exit the race prematurely. Even after negotiating the road sections, they still need to traverse the river, where much good work may be undone as the bed and passenger sink lower into the water, exhibiting an extreme case of bed-wetting! Finally reaching the end, the team can collapse on their bed – if it's still in one piece – and have a well deserved nap.

HISTORY

First conceived back in 1965 as a fundraiser, the race now has over 50 teams starting the contest ... although not everyone will finish in one piece. The first-ever race saw actual metal-framed hospital beds used, and competitors were then restricted to the Army, Navy and American Marines, with the latter again entering a team in 2006 dressed in Tarzan outfits.

A few teams fail to make it successfully to the end without some mishap, including one team who had a wheel fall off during the parade. With insufficient time to repair the bed, they decided to carry it instead and completed the race in an admirable 35 minutes. Another team decorated their bed with a twelve-foot-high kangaroo. However, police requested its removal from future races because of the time taken to get around the course. Every year there is a different theme to the event, and in 2006 one team dedicated their entry to the musical *The King and I*, with a Yul Brynner lookalike with arms crossed as passenger and six children dancing around the bed as they pushed it along.

The town of Knaresborough is twinned with Bebra in Germany, who enjoyed the event so much that they started their own bed race; while they themselves are twinned with the East German town of Friedrichroda, which stages a two-day bed race. No one has yet had the idea of jointly holding a 'twin bed' race!

ESSENTIALS

The bed race has two categories of entries, 'fast' and 'entertaining'. There is also a separate competition for non-racing beds, judged on appearance only. Make sure you enter the bed in the right category!

Teams must be aware of the large number of rules. For obvious reasons, every competitor must be able to swim, and there is a time limit of around 30 minutes for the beds to complete the course. Before the race, officials perform a safety inspection on the beds. There are precise requirements for the bed itself, including set dimensions of the wheels and frame, no king-sized beds or bunk beds allowed, and no mechanical aids, i.e. an engine. Also, don't forget to include a buoyancy aid for the river crossing. Pillows, mattress and a teddy bear are optional extras.

TIPS

There are two main issues to consider when entering the race. Runners should have a decent level of fitness to manage the killer hill, while the bed must be easy to manoeuvre. Having a very light passenger will also help the team get around the course in a fast time. Most use small children for this reason. For spectators, keep well back from the road as the beds move quickly and sometimes unpredictably.

WACKY FACT

One man walked across the river in stilts after the 2007 race was over, and has promised to perform a different act of wackiness every year.

IF YOU LIKE THIS

If a bed sounds too big, then you could always enter the Oxenhope Straw Race (see page 121), which requires competitors to carry or drag a bale of straw along a 2.5-mile course. Or, if you prefer to race baths instead of beds, enter the World Tin Bath Championships held on the Isle of Man every August.

WORLD PEA SHOOTING CHAMPIONSHIPS

'Puffed cheeks at the ready'

Location:	Witcham, near Ely, Cambridgeshire
Date:	Usually the second Saturday in July
Time:	Registration at 1pm for a 2pm start
Entry fee:	£1.50 per person (50p for juniors)
Further information:	www.witcham.org.uk
Grid reference:	TL 463 800

Spectator Fun:	★★
Wackiness:	★★★
World Champion:	★★★
Pain Factor:	★
Training Required:	★★★★
Family Friendly:	★★★

WHAT HAPPENS

This is one World Championship where naughty kids are the favourites to win, with adults desperately trying to remember from their misbehaving school days how to use the toy weapon.

Contestants require accuracy and a steady hand as they shoot dried peas towards a target twelve feet away, using only their lungs for power. The competition begins with everyone shooting five peas, all hoping to post a creditable score to take them through to the knockout stages. The target, made out of putty, consists of three rings, and a score of 1, 3 or 5 is awarded depending on whether the pea lands on the outer, middle or inner circle respectively. Peas that hit the target between two scores are assigned the higher score, while the pea itself does not have to remain embedded in the target to score, so long as it makes an indentation.

Competitors display a variety of techniques, and many betray a misspent childhood as they flawlessly fire the peas in quick succession into the middle of the target. Others fail miserably, with the peas barely managing to fall out of the shooter, often plopping out not far from where the competitor stood. Furthermore, novices mistake this for a pea eating contest as they struggle to manoeuvre the peas to the front of their mouth. Then there are those who naively attempt to place an over-sized pea into the shooter, often jamming one end and embarrassingly having to dislodge the pea while being watched by an amused crowd.

The highest sixteen scores progress to the knockout stage where competitors will go head to head. Alternate shots are taken at the target and the tension builds as the scores between the players remain close until the final pea has been shot. Even a good score at this stage can be in vain if the other player shoots close to the maximum possible score of 25 points. Any ties in the knockout stage will require a sudden death play-off. The winners of each match continue towards the grand final, where ten peas are shot.

HISTORY

The idea was conceived in 1971 after the local schoolmaster caught some children playing with pea shooters. This inspired him to turn the playground prank into a fundraising event at the village fair, to help raise funds towards a new village hall. Nowadays all proceeds contribute towards its maintenance.

The event has grown in popularity, attracting competitors from abroad, although the locals usually end up winning.

Entrants in previous years have resorted to dirty-handed tactics to ensure victory, including the use of laser shooters to maximise accuracy. Due to their success rate in subsequent championships, the organisers banned them from the main contest but added a specialist category for those who still wanted to exhibit their innovations. However, laser shooters were controversially re-introduced to the 2007 contest, causing much chagrin among the purists, and no prizes for guessing which type of shooter the winner used. There was even mention of one competitor threatening to bring a machine-gun pea shooter one year.

ESSENTIALS

At a small cost, competitors can purchase plastic shooters on the day, although many bring along their own shooter, providing it does not infringe any of the rules. The shooter can be made from any material, and can include sighting devices, but it should not exceed a length of twelve inches. Pea shooters must not be shared, and official peas are also provided. This is a very friendly event, perfect for the family, and there are several other games and attractions on the village green to entertain, should you suffer an early exit.

There is also a ladies' and a team category. As if they needed further opportunity for success, there is a separate contest for juniors, who stand between eight and ten feet from the target, dependent on age. But judging from their prowess in the past, maybe they should stand further back than the adults and be blindfolded!

TIPS

For absolute beginners: place one of the peas in the mouth, then, using the tongue to steer the pea to the back of the shooter, exhale sharply. When you become more proficient, try having all five peas in the mouth (don't swallow any), which means you can shoot them all at once without making adjustments; this is fine unless of course the first shot was off target. Finally, head to the practice area to refine your technique or seek advice from the experts – this is one wacky event where serious practice is essential if you want to win.

For perfect accuracy, consider the size and shape of the pea, which should be small enough to fit cosily inside the shooter, but not too loose; and the rounder the pea, the more aerodynamic. Maintain a tight grip on the shooter and remember to make adjustments for any wind.

(WACKY FACT)

Mike Fordham is in the Guinness Book of Records for winning the World Championship seven times. However, in 2006 a local woman, Sandra Ashley, had a clean sweep of all three titles, winning the ladies', open and team competitions. Unfortunately the quadruple, and winning the junior contest, was just too much to ask – no doubt she was pestered with pleas from children to reveal the secret of her success.

(IF YOU LIKE THIS)

Accuracy is also key in the World Black Pudding Throwing Championships held in Lancashire, which requires competitors to knock as many Yorkshire puddings as possible off a 30-foot-high platform using black puddings as projectiles.

TOTNES ORANGE RACES

*'Inspired by Sir Francis Drake, but not exactly
a game of bowls!'*

Location:	Fore Street, Totnes, Devon
Date:	A Tuesday in August
Time:	Races start 11am, with each age group run back-to-back with very short intervals
Entry fee:	Free
Further information:	Totnes Tourist Information, 01803 863168
Grid reference:	SX 801 604

Spectator Fun:	★★★
Wackiness:	★★★
Pain Factor:	★★
Training Required:	★
Family Friendly:	★★★★

WHAT HAPPENS

This is not a drinking contest, but competitors may require an aptitude for dribbling in a fruity alternative to the famous cheese rolling.

Contestants race down the steep high street in Totnes chasing an orange, starting from the Market Square and finishing 450 metres later at the Royal Seven Stars pub. First person to cross the finish line with an orange, not necessarily their own, is the winner. The catch ... the orange can only be kicked or thrown.

Several races take place throughout the morning, split according to age group, starting with the younger children and working up to adults who should know better. Each race contains around six participants, and locals dressed in Elizabethan costume harangue onlookers to enter. It's a case of the more the merrier for the crowd who line the narrow street, hopeful for some Grand Prix-type collisions early on. At the start, competitors delve into a box of oranges, taking pot luck on an orange that they hope will survive the journey to the bottom.

The starter offers some last-minute – and probably tongue-in-cheek – advice, requesting that the oranges remain in the middle of the road. Since this is a wacky event, competitors are unlikely to act responsibly, even if they try to. On the count of three, they're off and rolling, the oranges bowled low and hard, each immediately taking a random trajectory. Competitors futilely attempt to maintain eye contact with their orange as they begin the chase to catch up.

Carnage and confusion ensues as competitors and oranges become entangled. Unfortunately, there is nothing to stop

the entrants from pinching each other's oranges. In fact, with six oranges bunched up, nobody has any idea which one is theirs as everyone stumbles haphazardly down the street in blind pursuit, shouting to one another, 'Oi, that's my orange!'

Winning or losing the race depends on how the orange travels. Most competitors repeatedly bowl the orange, but this can be awkward, with many approaching the orange at an uncontrollable speed and hilariously misjudging the braking distance, losing valuable seconds as they clumsily backtrack.

Oranges tend to be thrown erratically, and over-eager spectators who stand perilously close to the oncoming action inevitably clash with the competitors who chase the oranges from side to side. It's not uncommon for oranges to become wedged in prams or to ricochet off an innocent bystander's body. The race has surprisingly avoided any serious injuries over the years (oranges usually come off worse for wear), although one year a first aid man became a reluctant participant.

The other tactic is to kick the orange, which allows the runner to maintain their downhill speed, but the foot method can be risky too. An orange that has split or exploded after an over-zealous kick will not be easy to move again, and can lead to an embarrassing climax for the competitor as they end the course orange-less, or with only a fragment of peel. Past winners have adapted the kicking action with a subtle side-foot rather than a reckless toe-poke.

Whatever technique is used, the halfway point is literally make or break for the orange, as the fastest speeds are reached. Throws or kicks become increasingly desperate (spectators should stand well back at this point) as competitors lose all coordination and battle to remain on two feet, or even one foot.

On the flat with the finish in sight, entrants zigzag across the road, losing speed with weary legs and slowly disintegrating oranges. The roar from the crowd provides much-needed motivation as they lurch forward for one final kick, sending the orange careering off the road for a final time. Competitors skid over the line in under two minutes, with a quick glance sideways to check they were not pipped at the post! The end is much welcomed, as bewildered competitors look back at the hill wondering why they are so knackered from running down it. Many complain of chest pains and double up in exhaustion, gasping for breath and complaining afterwards that the street was much longer than it was initially perceived ... and that's just the younger entrants.

HISTORY

The race has its roots firmly in the 16th century, but there seems to be no clear explanation of how the orange race was inspired. The most likely origin is that Sir Francis Drake bumped into a boy carrying a barrel of oranges (luckily it wasn't a barrel of pumpkins), causing the load to tumble down the hill with the boy in pursuit. Another suggestion is that the race commemorates the moment when Sir Francis Drake gave an orange to a local boy who, in later life, became Governor of Newfoundland.

ESSENTIALS

The first of the races involve the younger children, who sensibly race on a flat section, usually with parents in tow, if they can keep up. There is a very short interval between each of the adult races, so allow plenty of time to get to the start line. As well as the children's and adults' races, there is a special race, the Police Challenge, open to shopkeepers or uniformed people working in Totnes, but the police competitors probably have an advantage, given their 'peelers' nickname.

TIPS

The race has parallels with the hare and the tortoise story, where slow and steady is the key. Those who race off too quickly will inevitably pay for their temerity, as they spend more time retreating. The lack of rules usually means that the race deteriorates into a free-for-all, so anticipate plenty of orange-stealing as the faster runners retrieve the faster-rolling oranges. Accuracy is also important, and it's highly advisable to maintain a central position and avoid the gutter, but this is a lot harder than it sounds. For a touch of arrogance, consider deflecting the orange off the clock bridge, halfway along, although dropping the orange here would mean orange squash!

WACKY FACT

One year, an entrant won by running the race without his orange and then grabbing a substitute from a boy in the crowd.

IF YOU LIKE THIS

If this one is too tame, head off to Coopers Hill in Gloucestershire on Whit Monday – or maybe that should be twit Monday – for the cheese rolling races (see page 186). Unlike the orange race, the competitors take the battering, and once you start running you won't stop until the bottom ... we did warn you.

ROYAL MARINES COMMANDO CHALLENGE

'Mud, mud, glorious mud … just don't forget to bring some soap'

Location:	Bicton Arena, Woodbury Common, East Devon. Fifteen minutes east of Exeter
Date:	Saturday/Sunday in October
Time:	From early morning
Entry fee:	£17.50 per team member (plus minimum sponsorship)
Further information:	www.commandochallenge.co.uk
Grid reference:	SY 064 859

Spectator Fun:	★★★
Wackiness:	★
Pain Factor:	★★★★
Training Required:	★★★★
Family Friendly:	★★

WHAT HAPPENS

Royal Marines, known for their tough training, put teams through their paces on an 'endurance' course with a difference, involving numerous mud and water obstacles ... and all in the name of charity.

The three-mile course is one of four tests that Marine recruits must complete on their way to receiving the green beret. Unfortunately, the only thing competitors will be wearing at the end of the Commando Challenge will be layers of mud. Pumped up with fear, the teams literally hit the mud with the first of several demanding obstacles that will make or

break them, including various wet and very boggy sections intended to acclimatise competitors. Sadistic Marines loiter in the background, screaming insults and ensuring everyone becomes fully acquainted with the mud.

Teams must then face more daunting obstacles including scrambling up, and usually falling back down, the steep and slippery mud banks, wading through Peter's Pool, 50 metres of chest-high and freezing bog water, the knee-crunching tunnels which need no explaining and the Alligator Pit.

The crème de la crème of the course, the infamous Sheep Dip, is reserved until near the end, and is guaranteed to test even the toughest competitor. Competitors are pushed-pulled through one of two submerged two-metre-long tunnels, coming out the other side spouting much of the muddy water back out, and gasping for air. Plenty of 'pscychological bottle' is needed, but the Marines are on hand here to make sure you negotiate the obstacle safely – just don't get cold feet halfway through, and watch out for any sheep heading in the opposite direction.

In between the various obstacles, teams are expected to sprint, or at least disguise any signs of tiredness with a respectable jog (not always easy when wearing wet, heavy clothes), although when out of sight from the Marines, teams tend to grind to a stagger.

Exhausted and soaked to the bone, competitors begin the final assault, climbing a short muddy hill (what other type of hill is there!) on their hands and knees only. The unsympathetic Marines relentlessly drill the day recruits and take pleasure in commanding everyone to roll over in the mud as they make their way up towards the finish. Any clothing or skin that was clean, or at least not mud-coloured beforehand,

will be targeted, and those that find bathing in the mud beneath them will be offered a helping hand.

Teams finish the day covered head to toe in mud, but the tasks will encourage team bonding and nominated charities will be better off. The challenge is more about having fun than winning, for most people anyway, although there are prizes for the fastest teams.

HISTORY

The event was first organised back in 1990 by an ex-Marine as a three-mile endurance race and involved 80 competitors, raising £3,000 for charity.

In 1996 the seven-mile challenge was introduced, and in 2002 the event went international when a group of visiting

German Marines noticed the event on the internet and came down, even taking away the title. Since then, teams from Norway, the USA and New Zealand have all entered, with over 3,000 people taking part.

ESSENTIALS

There is a closing date for entries (usually 1 September) to allow the organisers to allocate team places, and the event is always over-subscribed, so enter early. There is also a minimum of three per team, but no maximum. Larger teams, however, means slower times, as each obstacle takes longer to negotiate. The event also attracts many female competitors, keen to show they are the better sex when it comes to getting dirty all over!

The minimum age is sixteen years and those under eighteen will need their parents to sign the dangerous events disclaimer. On a serious note, some of the obstacles are difficult and not for anyone with a dislike of dark, confined spaces; and it's recommended that arms and legs are covered to prevent too many cuts and scratches. It's not uncommon to see many bare chests, on the men, but as the event takes place in October the conditions may be wintry, and it's an arduous test for anyone without compounding the difficulties with the threat of pneumonia.

The event is not a fashion parade, so make wise sartorial choices. Avoid anything you want to wear again and choose clothes that will not weigh you down after rolling around in the mud a few times. Skips are available at the end for the filthy clothes, unless you want to take away a memento. There are showers, food and changing facilities at nearby Bicton Arena. Spectators are advised to park at the arena and make use of the regular shuttle bus out to the course.

Spectators should also note that it's almost impossible to stay clean, with tracks, trees and bushes dotted around the course all caked with mud. However, the beauty of this course is that you can follow the participants around and maybe develop an appetite to enter the following year.

TIPS

If you never liked cross country at school, then give this event a wide berth. Competitors are well advised to train seriously for the challenge so that they are able to navigate around the course after the initial run. It will not bode well for a team to start on the obstacles already out of breath, as each test will challenge even the fittest. Sensible footwear with high ankle support and plenty of grip should be worn, and tied on securely if you don't want to finish the course in bare feet. Finally, don't forget to warm up beforehand.

IF YOU LIKE THIS

After successfully completing the three-mile version, the following year's challenge is to tackle an extra four miles of road running on the seven-mile course, which the Marines use for training, although they also carry a military kit bag and rifle.

Try the Maldon Mud Race (www.maldonlions.co.uk/mudrace) in Essex, held every Christmas. This is pure mud, and requires competitors to run across an estuary and back at low tide, including wading through freezing water. The distance of 400 metres may not sound far, but don't underestimate the difficulties of running on soft mud. The average time is fifteen minutes and the main tip is: don't start at the back. After over 100 feet have trampled through the mud, the course will resemble a quagmire.

OXENHOPE STRAW RACE

'Competitors have a bale of a time!'

Location:	Oxenhope, near Keighley, West Yorkshire
Date:	First Sunday in July
Time:	Racing begins at midday until 3pm
Entry fee:	£25 per team of two
Further information:	www.strawrace.co.uk
Grid reference:	SE 032 348

Spectator Fun:	★★★
Wackiness:	★★
Pain Factor:	★
Training Required:	★★
Family Friendly:	★★★

WHAT HAPPENS

Another unique take on the pub crawl. Teams of two compete in a race on foot between two pubs. Sounds easy? Teams must also carry a bale of straw, negotiate various hazards and drink a pint of beer at several points along the course.

The straw race is a competitive but very friendly event contested by a staggering 200 teams. Teams drink their first beer at the Wagon and Horses pub on the outskirts of the Pennine village of Oxenhope before setting off in groups of three teams at one-minute intervals.

At each of the five scheduled stops along the 2.5-mile route, one pint of beer must be consumed by a team member, but the course is likely to increase in length if teams stop off for additional drinks and, inevitably, begin swerving and

zigzagging across the road. Female teams do things by halves, carrying only half a straw bale and drinking half pints, but there are no concessions for mixed teams – though male team members may grudgingly drink any beer left!

The first mile of the race is downhill (without the straw bale), and for the less competitive teams this is the only chance to put in some effort. The route takes teams off-road, running past a cemetery – no time for a lie down just yet – and then negotiating a couple of stiles, testing those who may have had a few beers before the race started. The obstacles will also provide an early challenge to those who entered in flamboyant fancy dress. A few years ago three men completed the entire course on cross-country skis, pulling the bale behind them. After struggling with the lack of snow, the last straw was surmounting the two stiles, and they wisely decided to take a detour, still completing the course within the allotted time.

At the first stop, the Bay Horse pub, teams down their second pint and then pick up their bale of straw using a variety of innovative, home-made vehicles to transport it to the finish … without cheating. The faster teams opt for a less cumbersome design that allows a quick pace, usually involving a couple of broomsticks tied together to hold the bale between them. A few competitors even begin carrying the straw bale on their shoulders, but it's a long way to the end using this technique. The slower teams resort to drag outfits and outrageous costumes to please the crowds and this excuses them from too much exertion!

Along the route, teams pass the bus station, providing an early temptation for the more devious teams to take a short cut, perhaps using the 'bale and ride' service! The bus station also marks the lowest point of the race – from here the only way is up.

The race takes in further drinks at three more stops, including the Shoulder of Mutton, which is no longer a public house but has now become a children's nursery. Just for the day, though, a drinks station is set up outside ... for over-18s only!

Live music en route provides much-needed motivation to the flagging competitors, while suspicious-looking spectators pose yet more hazards. Armed with buckets of water, they lurk along the course ready to pounce. The Lamb Inn, the third pub, is about halfway along the course. Apart from those determined to win, many choose to use this as a spot to recover some energy and delay the remainder of the race for as long as possible by taking an impromptu break.

Back on the road (a few hours later for some), weariness sets in as the hot July weather colludes with the weight of the

bale and the excess beer. Frequent toilet stops and tired legs slow the teams down to a shuffle. The bale begins to take on a more dishevelled appearance as teams become reckless with its transportation along the course, leaving the road back to the village strewn with loose straw. There are no rules regarding bale tampering, and the more mischievous teams 'accidentally' misplace part of the bale in order to lighten the load. The following day, bewildered drivers pass through Oxenhope wondering whether a barn blew up during the night!

Simply walking the route sober is difficult enough, but teams at the back still manage to remain buoyant as they edge up the final hill, often breaking into song to relieve the discomfort. Once the teams reach the finish at the Dog and Gun pub, they can gratefully ditch the straw bale, if any of it remains, continue drinking and enjoy the carnival atmosphere.

The fastest teams complete the course in around fifteen minutes and the slowest have three hours to finish. After this time, teams can continue and most do, but they will not receive an official result.

HISTORY

As usual, a chat in a pub spawned the idea of a charity race, and very soon they had come up with their own unique angle, with the first race in 1975. Over the years, all money raised has totalled an incredible £250,000. One man who had taken part for over 25 years even donated his wedding money to the Straw Race fund.

The race has since seen plenty of imaginative fancy dress, including one team running with a rickshaw made from the front end of a Fiat Uno. Another team called themselves 'Death by Chocolate' and were dressed as pall bearers, complete with a coffin full of chocolates which were thrown into the crowd, probably as a bribe to avoid being soaked.

Two men even decided to complete the course in snorkel, trunks and flippers – wonder if they took a quick plunge in the nearby reservoir? The race has missed only one year, in 2001, but as a substitute, imaginative organisers instead hired a steam train to raise money, calling it the Straw Race special.

ESSENTIALS

Registration for the race is on the Saturday or the Sunday before 10.30am. There are prizes for the winners, including one for the fastest veteran team and medals to all finishers. Teams of two can be male, female or mixed. For a small deposit of £10, the more competitive teams receive an official time; and to appease the physically challenged, or those just plain lazy, there are prizes for the best fancy dress.

While some teams do take the race seriously, the true essence is about having fun and raising sponsorship money. During the race itself, the road through the village is closed, but there is an official car park near the finish at the Dog and Gun, for a small charge. Shuttle buses are also provided to and from the railway station to the village.

TIPS

It's advisable to choose your partner wisely. The fastest team doesn't always win, and often it's a case of who can drink the quickest. One member of the team should run ahead to each drink station to put their order in, hopefully in time for the other person to arrive and gulp the beer down. Teams who wish to take the race seriously should tick the 'athlete' box on the entry form to ensure an early start, before the course clogs up with misplaced straw bales and competitors. Future entrants should also consider the hazards en route before deciding on their choice of attire.

IF YOU LIKE THIS

For a much bigger handicap, enter the Wrekin Barrel Race in Shropshire. Teams of four carry a nine-gallon beer barrel filled with water, not beer, along a course of 1.5 miles. If that isn't enough, the route ascends 1,000 feet to the top of Wrekin Hill ... and, more bad news, there are no beer stops along the way. Competitors can even attempt a solo effort with the same 50kg barrel, but straw racers may find the fun version more appealing, requiring teams to wear fancy dress and carry an empty barrel. Either way, with the start line in the old rifle range, competitors will want a quick getaway, and unfortunately, barrels cannot be rolled down the hill later on!

INTERNATIONAL BOGNOR BIRDMAN

'Those magnificent men in their flying machines, they go up, up, up, they go down, down, down ... but there are some who just go down!'

Location:	Worthing, West Sussex
Date:	Between July and September
Time:	From 1pm both days
Entry fee:	£50 (£75 for a team of two)
Further information:	www.birdman.org.uk
Grid reference:	TQ 149 023

Spectator Fun:	★★★
Wackiness:	★★★
Pain Factor:	★★★
Training Required:	★★★★
Family Friendly:	★★★

WHAT HAPPENS

Grab your wings and reach for the skies or you may end up looking very very silly.

The flying – or should that be plummeting? – takes place at the end of a pier, where competitors will leap off a 30-foot-high platform, aiming to travel as far as possible before making a splash. The competitor who manages the furthest distance wins the prestigious International Birdman Trophy.

There are three categories for the event: Condor, Leonardo da Vinci and the Kingfisher. The Condors have a realistic chance of flying, while the da Vinci class enter with high aspirations of becoming modern-day Orville Wrights, but their attempts inevitably conjure up images of Icarus, who experienced a completely different flying dilemma. The biggest crowd-puller of the weekend are the Kingfishers, who have very little hope of flying but instead tend to nose-dive, just like their ornithological namesakes.

Kingfishers enter the Birdman hoping to create the biggest laughs, with the most amusing entry plummeting away with the £500 prize. With no distances to decide the winner, judges instead consider the costume, props, the jump (including landing), and crowd applause. Plunging into the sea is optional, although everyone usually goes through with the jump.

Fancy dress is therefore a pre-requisite for success, with such past entrants as Batman, a skateboarding cow, a racehorse and even a condom that failed to demonstrate safe jumping. They also enter with names appropriately matching their flying pedigree, and in previous years the Comedy Seagull, the Flying Statue of Liberty and the Flatulent Fairies have all made a big splash.

Competitors have one minute on the pier for some improvisation, and many prance around the platform before jumping off in embarrassment. There are some, though, who arrive with a rehearsed mini-performance, before reluctantly trundling towards the edge of the platform and, with a brief hesitation, stepping off the edge without even trying to achieve a creditable distance. Some do attempt a futile run-up, but either way they end up resembling a doomed cartoon character as they drop like a stone, managing no more than two or three metres before the inevitable splash. In addition to the overall winner, the funniest moment in the Kingfisher section wins the Lins Trophy.

The da Vinci class are home-made, innovative designs that look as if they could fly but, more often than not, fail miserably. Unlike the Kingfishers, they take their entry very seriously. Their flying machines have eccentric designs with apt names such as the Skycopter and the human-powered Ornithopter.

Spectators expecting rocket or catapult-propelled inventions, or the use of balloons to aid ascent, will be disappointed. However, beyond these technical restrictions, competitors can design their entry to be as audacious and inventive as they desire.

Making the most of the run-up, they take a leap of faith and pray that their entry remains airborne at least long enough to retain some credibility. The last thing they want is to turn up with a streamlined and expensive-looking machine only to mimic the Kingfisher entrants.

The Condor class, the most serious category, attracts competitors from aeronautic backgrounds including aircraft designers, aerospace engineers and flying instructors. Entries are often expensive-looking and are usually based on modified hang-gliders. After maximising the run-up distance, they jump off the edge, hopefully clearing the scaffolding, before gliding through the air. The distance measured is to where they hit the water, and many will battle with their contraption to skim the surface as long as possible, preferably for around ten seconds, before finally giving up.

The two main flying categories have attempts on both days. The furthest flight scores twelve points, second place gets ten points and so on. Scores are cumulative and the best score amassed over the weekend flies off with the International Birdman trophy.

Besides winning their own category, there is a financial incentive to enter the Condor or da Vinci class; whoever flies beyond 100 metres will win the jackpot prize of £30,000. However, the record still stands at 89.2 metres and it will require an ingenious entry and favourable weather conditions for a competitor to manage a greater distance. Should a Kingfisher ever collect this award, there will doubtless be a drug test.

HISTORY

The neighbouring resort of Selsey first staged the contest (then known as the Birdman Rally) back in 1971, where they jumped off the RNLI ramp. Seven years later the event outgrew the resort and moved to Bognor, with a higher platform and greater chance to win the jackpot.

In 2003, Virgin Atlantic sponsored the event and Richard Branson flew in for the occasion, but unfortunately he was unable to enter one of his planes into the contest! Anyone can take part in the madcap event, as proved the following year when a blind competitor entered the contest.

Sadly, part of Bognor pier was demolished in 2008 and health and safety concerns meant that the event could no longer take place in the town. Fortunately, nearby Worthing stepped in and had the honour of hosting the 30th contest. It's not yet known where the 2009 contest will take place.

ESSENTIALS

The event is always oversubscribed, so enter early to guarantee one of the 30 or so places. For the Kingfisher category, entries which sound funnier are more likely to be chosen to participate. All participants must be able to swim at least 50 metres and, obviously, not suffer from vertigo. For those who still worry about their landing, a safety boat is on hand to fish entrants out of the water.

The tide governs the flying times, with a minimum of six metres water depth required. Wind speeds exceeding twenty knots will delay the competition. There is a full list of rules and regulations available with the application form. Registration for all contestants is between 7am and 11am on both days.

The event attracts over 30,000 spectators, with the main road along the promenade closed during the contest. Fortunately, a large screen offers those without binoculars a close-up view of the action. Besides the winner of each of the three classes, there is an additional prize, the Leaderboard Time Challenge, for the contestant who stays in the air the longest. The winner receives £30 for every second they remain airborne to a maximum purse of £1,000 for at least twenty seconds. Finally, there is a Wings badge for any competitor who manages to set a distance further than that achieved by the athlete who leaps off the pier at the beginning of the day.

TIPS

For budding Condors or da Vinci entries, it helps to have an aeronautical background, and hang-gliding experience is of course essential. If you are not going to fly far, then at least make sure you look good, but be careful how far you go to stand out. In 2006, Steve Preston (aka Stupid Steve) entered the Kingfisher section wearing a costume of tar and feathers. Unfortunately, removing the costume was a lot harder than expected and Steve suffered a sticky drive home!

WACKY FACT

In 1989, well known Winter Olympian Eddie 'the Eagle' Edwards managed to 'ski jump' eleven metres off the pier.

IF YOU LIKE THIS

Ilfracombe in North Devon stages a similar event every August, albeit on a much smaller scale. Further afield, the Bognor Birdman has even spawned a similar event in China! For a different kind of daredevil experience, why not throw yourself off a hill while chasing a cheese at Cooper's Hill, Gloucestershire?

ATHERSTONE BALL GAME

*'There are no goals, the winner gets a police escort
and even the Navy are too afraid to return'*

Location:	Atherstone, Warwickshire
Date:	Shrove Tuesday
Time:	3pm
Entry fee:	None
Further information:	Atherstone Tourist Information 01827 712395
Grid reference:	SP 308 978

Spectator Fun:	★★
Wackiness:	★
Pain Factor:	★★★★
Family Friendly:	★

WHAT HAPPENS

A 'no-holds-barred' footballing tradition where it's a case of every man for himself. Just don't expect the ball to get much action. The game takes place in the high street of Atherstone, and as a sign of things to come, all the shopkeepers spend the morning boarding up their windows and doors!

Before the start of the main action, local dignitaries gather on the balcony on the first floor of one of the town's banks and throw sweets and pennies down to the children below. This is probably a bribe so that they clear off to leave only the foolhardy in the street for the football game. A gold coin is also thrown down into the crowd, supposedly to uphold a tradition going back to the 12th century when the teams fought for a bag of gold.

As 3pm approaches, the younger children reluctantly retreat from the street and are replaced by menacing-looking teenagers and adults, loitering with intent. After several tense minutes, the ball is finally dropped from the balcony straight into the ruck of players below, all with their arms outstretched, hopeful of making the initial catch. The leather ball is about 27 inches across and weighs four pounds, made specially for the event and filled with water so that players are unable to kick it too far, though in 2007 the ball was filled with air. There are three coloured ribbons (red, white and blue) attached to the ball before the game starts, and each player who manages to tear off a ribbon after kick-off (and keep hold of it) will receive £10. Sometimes a fourth, black ribbon is added as a mark of respect for the passing of a local player or spectator.

The ball descends deep into the scrum, and thereafter the game becomes a melee with no rules and no goals. While there are no teams to speak of, players work in smaller units to keep hold or gain possession of the ball. For the first hour or so, the game takes place in good spirits and the younger or less physical players (and even a few women) can involve themselves without too much risk of injury, with the onus on as many people as possible touching the ball.

Whenever the ball does break free, usually as a consequence of a small knock or kick, the player receiving the ball has little option other than to boot the ball back up the street. Participants can attempt to carry the ball, but given the number of people hemmed into the narrow street, this is

clearly not an option. About 40 people take part at any one time and the play swings from one end of the street to the other.

The aim of the game is to be the player holding the ball at 5pm, and into the last 30 minutes the tempo of the game suddenly changes as players bully for possession. Locals are not afraid to use aggression, and with no referee officiating there are several skirmishes, which compensates for the directionless feel to the game. As with other similar traditions, the game is also an opportunity for players to strike a blow to avenge an incident that may have occurred during the previous year. Any locals who have been up to no good and upset a few players in recent months may decide wisely to give the game a wide berth.

With about ten minutes left on the clock, the ball will suddenly stop moving and disappear deep inside one final scrum. The player with the ball will end up jammed into the corner of the street, surrounded by his supporters (usually it's predetermined which players will keep the ball at the end). Often the ball is burst for ease of gripping. Now and again opposition players will launch an attack, climbing over the crowd to inch closer to the ball, but inevitably a raised fist or foot will warn them away. Repeated attempts to steal the ball are in vain, and at the end, from the mass of players, the stewards seek out the winner who then gratefully receives a police escort to the Angel Inn to collect his prize. Weary players hobble off home, grateful that they can abstain from violent ball games for 40 days and nights!

HISTORY

Exact dates of such traditions are always vague, but it probably first took place about 800 years ago during the reign of King John. Such is the passion in Atherstone that the game continued throughout both world wars and even avoided abandonment during the foot and mouth crisis in 2001 because the game was confined to the town only.

The game was originally a match between Warwickshire and Leicestershire, but these days the teams are smaller and harder to spot. Today's game is restricted to Long Street, whereas in the past, play covered the whole town, which meant the odd excursion into the canal (with players and the ball getting soaked) and over the walls of a workhouse, where inmates had a brief kick around. Sadly, the smaller pitch also precludes any smuggling antics, which have brought proceedings to a humorous and abrupt halt in the past. One year, the smugglers even had the audacity to hold the ball to ransom, using the local newspaper as intermediary.

The thrower of the ball at the start has often been a job for a high-profile celebrity, with Larry Grayson, George Formby and Ken Dodd all at one time assisting. The latter had a narrow escape in 1970 when the balcony scaffolding he was standing on collapsed by a few feet, requiring him to jump back through the window.

ESSENTIALS

There is a delegation of stewards on hand should anyone become a reluctant player, with a police presence for backup. Minor injures (bloodied noses, black eyes etc ...) are considered part of the tradition and go unpunished, although a major fracas in 1986 very nearly ended the game for good. As with other events, if you don't want to be dragged into the game, stand well back. The best vantage points are from buildings on the high street, so it's best to make friends with the storekeepers or book a room in the hotel. Don't forget to park your car well away from the action – one year, competitors decided to overturn a car to stop the game heading down a side street.

TIPS

This is a very enjoyable event to watch, but those taking part are normally local men and women who expect some pain and suffering. Equally, watching the event can be just as dangerous, as the scrum can move randomly and surprisingly quickly.

(WACKY FACT)

Sailors from HMS *Atherstone* once turned up, wearing T-shirts emblazoned with the slogan 'We're taking the ball back with us!' They went away empty-handed, with fewer clothes than they started with.

(IF YOU LIKE THIS)

The Ashbourne Royal Shrovetide Football Game takes place on Shrove Tuesday and Ash Wednesday in nearby Derbyshire. Those with fewest war wounds can therefore try a whole different ball game the day after, but in Ashbourne the pitch is three miles long, so definitely not for those still recovering from their antics in Atherstone.

MINCE PIE EATING CONTEST

'A contest to get your teeth into ... just skip the main course'

Location:	Wookey Hole, Somerset
Date:	A Tuesday in November
Time:	Midday
Entry fee:	None

Further information:
www.wookeyhole.co.uk/thebigeat

Grid reference:	ST 531 476

Spectator Fun:	★★
Wackiness:	★★
World Champion:	★★
Pain Factor:	★★★
Training Required:	★★★★
Family Friendly:	★★

WHAT HAPPENS

Intestinal fortitude is stretched to its limits as gutsy competitors must wolf down as many festive mince pies, and that's without cream, as possible within a ten-minute period. But with a mouth-watering first prize of £1,000, the winner will be hoping that's the only big figure they'll be walking away with!

After resisting the temptation of the café tantalisingly located next to the venue, a maximum of twelve hungry contestants arrive on stage, all sporting extra-large, vomit-coloured T-shirts dished out by officials – perhaps a last-minute warning for those taking part! The first tactics of the competition soon come into play with the drinks order. Novices plump for water, unaware of the benefits of fizzy drinks, which are the popular choice among the more experienced entrants. Apparently, the gas created from the fizzy drink expands the stomach enough to accommodate an extra mince pie or two – obviously, there are negligible seconds lost to burping!

Various physiques assemble on stage, some looking considerably more qualified for the event, those with larger beer bellies justifiably earning the favourites' tag. In turn, the compere grills each contestant on their credentials for taking part and then prompts a guess on their expectations, which range from the ultra-cautious to the downright foolhardy. Finally, the rules are read out, and entrants are reminded that a large bucket is available behind them should they feel the urge of a 'reversal', turning the event into a throwing-up contest.

Standing within grasp of a plate of 50 mince pies (more can be requested), nervous competitors brace themselves for some insane eating, while holding back the butterflies in the stomach to accommodate more pies. The first few minutes see mouths stuffed effortlessly with mince pies, the swallowing keeping up with the fast tempo of the dance music played in the background. Two bites are sufficient for the first pie to vanish without hitting the sides. In between each munch, competitors overcome the dry texture of the pastry by gulping down liquid. Luckily, the contest lasts only ten minutes – any longer could see many entrants heading off to the toilets in disqualification.

The disparity between expectation and reality hits home about the halfway mark, with signs of discomfort and sighs of resignation across the stage as appetites fail to stretch to double figures. Many entrants accept that they don't have the stomach for the contest, instead idly fondling the mince pies with the occasional nibble. If you can't eat, you can't, no matter how much you want to, and cautious competitors allow

common sense to intervene, abstaining before one too many pies sends them heading towards the bucket. The leaders, meanwhile, encourage the onset of middle-age spread and relentlessly bolt down pie after pie in a stomach-churning feat of epic proportions.

The closing stages find the contenders faced with new problems, with aching jawbones after relentless chewing and grinding. Not even the music can motivate the competitors now, who enter mince pie meltdown and consume at a pace more akin to the waltz as the drinking begins to dominate proceedings.

The final countdown is much welcomed and sees a resurgence among the ailing competitors, who feel their competitive streak once more, grudgingly quickening the scoffing. Chewing and swallowing can continue beyond the allotted time, and nearly everyone takes the opportunity to push one final pie into their orifice, before gritting their teeth and hoping that the last mouthful stays down, avoiding premature ejection!

As the count-up begins, contestants stand back, belly flopping to the floor, in urgent need of indigestion tablets. Others give a rewarding pat to their tummy after a productive ten minutes and wait optimistically for the result, but many know beforehand that they have failed abysmally. As the competitors stagger off, sadistic officials announce that free lunches are available in the cafeteria – but are very confident that there will be few takers. The last thing on competitors' minds is a steak and kidney pie, although in 2006 the winner had just that for dessert. Not surprisingly, none of the participants bother to take home any of the uneaten mince pies.

Unwittingly perhaps for the winner, first prize also includes a trip to the USA to participate in another eating contest, where they will be up against experienced professionals.

HISTORY

In 2006, the contest was the first official competitive eating event held in the UK that was subject to the rules of the international body (or should that be stomach?) of competitive eating, the IFOCE (www.ifoce.com). The inaugural event featured Sonya 'The Black Widow' Thomas from the USA, who managed an incredible 46 mince pies, which works out at nearly five a minute. Implausibly, Sonya is also rake-thin, a physique which supposedly encourages intense eating, with less fat to restrict the stomach's expansion when under pressure. For the average competitor, it would be nigh-impossible to attempt to attain Sonya's build while training to be a competitive eater.

ESSENTIALS

The mince pies are cooked by a local bakery and are also suitable for vegetarians, with a very tasty shortcrust pastry containing delicious mincemeat – but try telling that to the competitors afterwards. Competitors will be disqualified if they are sick during or straight after the contest, although many professionals do use the Roman method, whereby they purposely vomit in private to keep their sodium levels down.

Entry is via the website, but with a maximum of twelve contestants it's advisable to apply well in advance. The application requests further information on your eating credentials – the wackier the better in order to secure a place. The website, www.oa.org, caters for overeaters anonymous, something most competitive eaters will definitely need access to!

TIPS

Beforehand, walk around to build up an appetite, and drink plenty of water to stretch the stomach and rein in those hunger pangs. During the contest itself, speed is the only factor. Keep slamming down as much food as possible before the brain sends signals to the stomach to say 'Hold the pies'.

The 2007 winner, Clive Pearson, knelt down to scoff his mammoth effort of 26 pies ... was this a posture facilitating rapid digestion or a ploy to save crucial seconds by being closer to the action? He also adopted the drink-pie-drink tactic to prevent the pastry clogging the mouth up, but admitted afterwards he was no longer fond of mince pies!

Techniques often used by professionals include moving around on the spot to burn up some of the food as they go, and even the ridiculous use of protective eyewear. Daft as it sounds, flying pieces of over-cooked pastry lodging under your eyelid will require immediate attention and may lose you precious seconds. Contestants may also consider skipping the chewing stage and swallowing the mince pies whole ... just check that someone close by is able to perform the Heimlich procedure in case things go a bit pie-shaped!

WACKY FACT

Professionals have trained their eating habits to devour food whole or adopted one of many well-known techniques, including the chipmunk approach, where food is stuffed into both cheeks while continuing to eat. Hot dog eating champion Takeru Kobayashi has taken competitive eating to extremes and expanded his stomach capacity over time with a regime of exercise and drinking large volumes of water. Takeru can now ignore any signs of feeling full and eat as much as he wants. Let's hope he doesn't ever enter the contest.

IF YOU LIKE THIS

A few weeks later, Harry's Bar in Wigan, Lancashire hosts the World Pie Eating Championship (see page 232), where the winner is the fastest to eat a single, but very chunky, pie. For those with a new-found talent, head to the USA, where face-stuffing is considered a profession. To give you an appetite, here are some current world records to strive for:

Pickled jalapenos – 177 in fifteen minutes
Doughnuts (cream-filled) – 47 in five minutes
Pizza – 22 slices in ten minutes

WORLD STONE SKIMMING CHAMPIONSHIPS

'Stone me!'

Location: Easdale Island, near Oban, Argyll and Bute

Date: A Sunday in September

Time: 11am registration for 12pm start

Entry fee: £4 for three skims (2007)

Further information: www.stoneskimming.com

Grid reference: NM 740 169

Spectator Fun: ★★★

Wackiness: ★★★

World Champion: ★★

Pain Factor: ★

Training Required: ★★★

Family Friendly: ★★★★

WHAT HAPPENS

First contested a 'stone age' ago by the island's slate workers, the World Championships now attracts hundreds of 'stone crazy' competitors.

Stone skimming, also known as skiting, is the art of throwing a 'flattish' stone across the surface of a body of water and attempting to bounce it as many times as possible. However, because of the impossible task of counting skims once a stone begins to aquaplane, an ability to skim will not be enough to make you World Champion on Easdale Island. Instead, so long as the stone has managed three skims, it's the distance travelled that counts. This of course means that a stone can skim 100 times but still not win!

The skimming arena lies within a disused slate mine, marked off by two lines of buoys about twenty metres apart. The stone must remain within this area, with automatic

disqualification for any that stray outside, no matter how good the skim is. Judges line the side of the arena, standing on the quarry edge, and measure an approximate distance. A further judge stands at the start, armed with a green and a red flag, deciding whether the throw is valid.

The location itself offers a further dilemma, in that the far end of the quarry is just a stone's throw away, at 63 metres, which precludes any future contestants breaking the record – although there have been tongue-in-cheek suggestions to extend the quarry. Should more than one competitor hit the wall, there is a play-off. This happened in 2006, when the eventual winner even managed to repeat the feat.

To the chorus of 'toss on', the contest begins with the children. After delving into the bucket of stones, the youngsters stand on a podium just short of the water's edge. A few of the younger entrants exhibit a natural talent and nonchalantly skim the stone a creditable distance (often beating the men and women), but the majority, with half-hearted swings, struggle to manage more than one splash. A few even threaten to follow the stone into the water with their over-enthusiastic launch.

The judges shout out the distances of each skim back to the official at the start, but under the howling gales often blowing in from the sea, the measurements may be misheard. One wonders whether former champions have been incorrectly declared after a stone-deaf official wrote down the wrong distance!

The men and women limber up with a few stretches before taking the podium. Women are up first but fail to post any big throws, but at least they have the technique to register a distance. After the first few skims for the men, it becomes evident that skimming is not as easy as it sounds. Many embarrassingly fail to skim more than once, instead going for power and consequently managing only a single splash, but they succeed better than those who completely miss the arena.

The more experienced skimmers often see their precise efforts met with disappointment, as the stone initially flies optimistically towards the quarry wall before a sudden breeze whips up, deflecting the stone just out of bounds. The competitor eyes the official hopefully, but inevitably receives the red flag.

A few competitors cockily arrive on the podium rejecting the local slate, instead clutching hand-picked 'foreign' stones. They still have a nervous moment when the official verifies the size of the stone and gleefully discards any rule-breaking skimmers (those exceeding three inches) back into the water, to the dismay of the competitor who must now trawl through the bucket.

Competitors inch closer to the back wall as the day progresses, exhibiting ever more elaborate postures as they bend further to the floor before launching the stone or deftly flicking their wrist to spin it (which apparently prevents it from tipping sideways). Other skims hit the buoys with a clang, to the crowd's amusement, thereby losing the extra four or five metres that could make the stone a winner.

Finally, towards the end, the favourites begin to appear and there is a massive roar as a skim finally goes as far as is physically possible, and with a faint noise of the stone nicking the far end of the quarry, the judge jubilantly shouts back to the crowd: 'Back wall!'

HISTORY

The contest first took place back in 1983 when the island was populated by slate workers, but the World Championships were run in their current form only from 1997 onwards. The event usually attracts fancy dress, including three Elvis impersonators in 2006 who even managed to mimic the Elvis stance when they threw. Competitors are often so excited that they strip off before having their three skims ... perhaps mishearing the officials when they shout 'Skim off', or maybe they're contemplating going for a 'skimmy-dip'!

Make sure you remain within the quarry when throwing. In recent contests, two competitors have managed the near-impossible feat of not only missing the water but also the quarry itself, both launching the stone almost at 90 degrees towards the crowd. One stone narrowly missed a spectator's head and finished up in the sea, but on the other occasion, the stone did hit somebody in the crowd ... luckily that year the culprit was a woman!

ESSENTIALS

The contest takes place in the middle of two quarries, sitting alongside the Atlantic Ocean. The smaller of the quarries acts as a suitable practice area for novices, but you will need to find your own skimmers, if there are any left at all! Competition stones come from a 'secret' location elsewhere on the island and are well guarded until the skimming begins. Besides the main winner's trophy, the best female entrant receives the Sea-fair Salver and all the juniors win a prize regardless of how well they skimmed. The best local junior is awarded the Bertie, in honour of the event's founder.

Easdale Island is accessible by a five-minute passenger ferry from the mainland (£1.50 for adults and 75p for children), and you pay on the return journey, so make sure you have enough change, otherwise it's a long swim home! Then again, the island's charm and scenery may persuade you to stay longer anyway.

There's a pre-skim party the night before, offering a BBQ, music and a chance to meet fellow competitors and discuss tactics. Just make sure you wake up stone cold sober for the contest. Unfortunately, there's no accommodation on the island (unless you can befriend the locals) or on the immediate mainland.

(**TIPS**)

Stone skimming is one of the more intricate wacky sports, in which stone selection and technique are just as important as brute strength. Slate is the ideal stone and the preferred shape is triangular, thin and flat with a slight concavity, but if it's too light it could blow away. The best skimmers usually aim for their first skim at the 30 metres mark. Skimming the stone into the water too soon will sap its momentum, while over-shooting the stone will expose it to the wind, often blowing it out of range.

Serious contenders for the title who wish to prepare that bit more than their rivals should consider the scientific research by Frenchman Lyderic Bocquet. He proved the optimum angle for entry of the stone into the water to be 26 degrees ... just don't forget to bring your protractor! Furthermore, if you can also launch the stone faster than 25mph, at a spinning speed of fourteen times a second, while accounting for gravity and with an ounce of beginner's luck, then you have a very good chance of winning.

For those desperate for success and low enough to stoop to cheating, drilling tiny holes in the stone will reduce the water drag and thus make the stone skim further. This is why golf balls have dimples, although you may attract suspicion on the start line as you reach for your cordless power drill!

WACKY FACT

The world record for Stone Skipping (as they say in the USA) is 51 skims and is currently held by Russell Byars, carrying the stone an incredible 250 feet. His stance is similar to that of a baseball pitcher, with an exaggerated follow-through.

IF YOU LIKE THIS

There are two other stone skimming contests held in the UK. 2007 saw the inaugural Welsh Open Stone Skimming Championships in Pembrokeshire, where the same rules apply as in the World Championships, but which also includes a team event. Meanwhile, in Brighton, Sussex, there is the John Lidbetter All-Weather Open International Stone Skimming Competition. Taking place in the sea, the contest is decided by the actual number of skims ... as long as the stones don't get too rough a ride!

MAPLETON BRIDGE JUMP

'Something to kick the year off in style, but ending with a New Year resolution never to take part again!'

Location:	Mapleton, near Ashbourne, Derbyshire. Watch out for signs outside Ashbourne
Date:	New Year's Day
Time:	Midday
Entry fee:	None
Further information:	Okeover Arms, 01335 350305
Grid reference:	SK 165 479

Spectator Fun:	★★★
Wackiness:	★★
Pain Factor:	★★★
Training Required:	★★
Family Friendly:	★★★

(**WHAT HAPPENS**)

The scenic village of Mapleton, on the edge of the Peak District, boasts one of the coldest rivers in the UK. It also proudly hosts the biggest bridge jump in the country (and ultimate hangover cure) when on New Year's Day a small number of reluctant competitors, some with trepidation, take a leap of faith and brave the icy waters in the name of charity.

The bridge jump is actually the midway point of a race which begins on the water and finishes with a dash to the pub. Teams of two begin by launching a plastic kayak into the River Dove and then proceed to paddle furiously down the river over a distance of around 1km.

The race is a mass start, but teams soon spread out with the fittest, or those less hungover, opening up a gap. The back markers perhaps purposely move along more slowly, clinging to the faint hope that once they reach the bridge everyone will have gone home. One year, one member of a team was even discovered walking alongside his boat on the bank of the river, after entering the race despite not being able to swim. Who knows what he made of the bridge jump?

After an easy straight stretch along the river, a weir, with a ten-foot drop into a plunge pool, provides an early hazard to the boats. From here, the river becomes more treacherous, with hidden rocks and small waterfalls offering further resistance to the teams' efforts to navigate down safely. A final waterfall requires teams to stay to the right, before easing their boat on to a shingle beach. The teams leap out of their boat and sprint back on to dry land, towards Okeover Bridge.

Before the event grew too big, devious officials would sail a mini pirate ship towards the leading teams and pelt them with eggs, or even hose them down, thus giving the slower teams a fighting chance.

Around 1,000 spectators line both sides of the river, ready to witness the first of many lemmings jumping off the bridge. Climbing a short ladder, competitors perch themselves precariously on the edge, one hand firmly gripping the side, as they peer down towards the icy waters just under 30 feet below. With just a brief moment to question their sanity, they psych themselves up before plunging feet-first into the water, around eight feet deep. The narrowness of the river requires pinpoint accuracy. On hitting the water, competitors find themselves briefly submerged before popping up and gasping for breath. Freezing temperatures in the river send shock

© Ashbourne News Telegraph

waves throughout the body, but at least their hangover has miraculously vanished.

Those in pursuit arrive very soon after the leaders jump, and wait in a queue, urging those in front to hurry up. Many competitors throw themselves off the bridge without any hesitation, while some of the first-timers stand physically and mentally frozen at the top, focusing on the jump and contemplating their rashness. Inevitably, even the most anxious competitor makes the plunge into the water below to a chorus of cheers. One year, a competitor required several failed countdowns from the crowd before finally loosening her grip and dropping straight down.

Other teams tackle the jump humorously (without breaking the safety rules), attempting a variety of acrobatics in midair to impress the crowd. Anyone jumping irresponsibly, e.g. head-first or backwards, will be disqualified and is likely to require the services of the first aid tent. Fortunately, there are divers on hand in the water to ensure that all jumps are completed successfully.

As soon as they have overcome the shock of the freezing-cold water, competitors muster enough energy to swim to the other side of the river, spurred on by the fear of their limbs seizing up. After clambering out with chattering teeth and goose-bumps from head to foot, they run the final leg across a field, about 500 yards, towards the village pub. The winning time is around the fifteen-minute mark, and, not surprisingly, the first thing on their mind is a hot shower.

HISTORY

A joke in the pub between two friends spurred a father, with his son and friends, to jump off the bridge one sunny day. Later that year, locals challenged them to repeat the jump, only this time the river was considerably chillier. They agreed to do it during the festive season, choosing New Year's Day as the appropriate time. In the first year of the race, the organiser even went on the radio, and when asked whether there was a winner's trophy, appropriately replied, 'the brass monkey award'. Unfortunately, no such trophy existed and his apprentice hastily sculpted a monkey-shaped award from a piece of brass using a hacksaw.

This was over twenty years ago, and since then the event has evolved into a race, but the jump remains the main attraction. Over the years, the race has seen a variety of boat designs. Originally, there were teams of three, who competed in rafts constructed from old barrels. These were replaced by wooden and then more resilient metal designs. The latter were less successful, though, and teams often capsized due to the boat's heaviness and awkwardness to steer. The current plastic boats are much more streamlined, safer, and hopefully unbreakable, given their price tag of around £250 each.

Spectators have also seen a fair number of surprises. A few years ago, a female competitor jumped off the bridge wearing only a T-shirt. As she flew through the air, it rose over her head, revealing more goose-bumps than perhaps she bargained for.

In previous years, the organisers permitted spectators to jump from the bridge, but due to rising insurance costs this is no longer possible.

ESSENTIALS

This event is open only to a limited number of teams, due to the available boats, with local teams normally given priority. It's therefore recommended to book a boat well in advance to have any hope of participating, and outsiders may wish to bribe the organiser for a chance to take part. There are also reserve teams waiting to replace anyone who drops out. 2008 will see the first-ever ladies-only race, with about six teams, and the men's race has now grown to incorporate twenty teams.

An ability to swim is a pre-requisite for entry. Vertigo sufferers should obviously keep well away from the race unless they are looking for something more lasting than a cure for a hangover. The best place to observe the race is on either side of the river, next to the bridge. There's plenty of parking on the road leading to Mapleton, but avoid the village itself.

TIPS

To have any chance of winning, teams need to be near the front when they reach the bridge. With only a short run to the finish, it would require a very fast sprint to overtake any other teams. However, there is the opportunity for some gamesmanship, as competitors jump in the order that they reach the bridge, regardless of which team they belong to. If members of teams in the chasing pack can sandwich themselves between the leaders, this may slow them down sufficiently to leave a closer run at the end. Since both team members must cross the finish line for the result to count, this is a worthwhile tactic.

Choose clothing to fit the extreme conditions and avoid wearing a baggy top, as this may balloon up and make it difficult to swim. Trunks or a bikini will definitely be a crowd-pleaser and guarantee a fast swim! To prepare for the shock of the jump, entrants may consider taking cold showers for a few weeks leading up to the race, and a liberal coating of Vaseline over the body will ease the shock of the plunge.

IF YOU LIKE THIS

For a much warmer plunge, teams of four can compete in the World Water Bombing Championships, taking place at Ponds Forge swimming pool, Sheffield. Points are awarded for style and costume, but it's really all about making the biggest splash.

WORLD CRAZY GOLF CHAMPIONSHIPS

'Expect more seagulls than eagles!'

Location:	Hastings, East Sussex
Date:	A weekend in late October
Time:	Both days from 10.30am. Prize-giving is at 4pm on the Sunday
Entry fee:	£25 for six rounds of golf (plus £15 membership)
Further information:	www.worldcrazygolf.co.uk
Grid reference:	TQ 821 093

Spectator Fun:	★★
Wackiness:	★
World Champion:	★★
Pain Factor:	★
Training Required:	★★★★
Family Friendly:	★★

WHAT HAPPENS

With a first prize of £1,000, the World Crazy Golf Championships may have the wackiest name, but it's arguably the most seriously contended event on the wacky circuit. Located within a putter's throw of the sea, where one bad shot can mean a sandwedge for the second – not even Tiger Woods can win this one!

Competitors play three rounds on both the crazy golf course and the not-so-crazy, but trickier, mini-golf. The event attracts a variety of characters, from teenage prodigies to first-timers, and must be the only contest where international players compete alongside no-hopers!

After some last-minute practice, competitors assemble for a clarification of the rules and allocation of teams. On day one, everyone plays in groups of three and scores for each other. Each group contains at least one expert, on hand to share their knowledge and provide tips to the novice, unless of course they start getting envious of any beginner's luck.

The crazy golf course is where players go for broke, aiming for as many aces (holes in one) as possible. Each hole has its own gimmick, including windmills (watch out for the moving sails), obelisks and waterwheels, besides many awkwardly-placed ditches, bunkers and ramps. For the initial tee-off (not a cue to put the kettle on), players place their ball anywhere within a set area, where hole-in-one shots are possible only if the ball begins on an exact spot. Close examination of certain holes reveals indents or suspect markers, and the more devious competitor may be tempted to add a few markers of their own to confuse others.

The serious contenders play shots with no margin for error, aiming through the eye of a needle to get the precise angles, or rebounding off two walls so that the ball just drops into the hole. As they nonchalantly pick up the ball, other players gawp at the shot in awe and make a mental note for their next round.

Beginners are far more amusing to watch as they negotiate the crazy golf with a gung-ho attitude, and for every fluke or slice of luck there will be an horrendous hole just around the corner. First-timers confidently tee off only to see a nasty ricochet placing the ball further back than where it began, or more embarrassingly, lodging the ball deep inside one of the course obstacles. It's highly unusual for a lost ball to be reported in crazy golf, but not impossible.

Where crazy golf rewards daring play, the mini-golf course requires copious skill and judgement. Most holes offer a straight line to the flag, but throw in a few bumps and slopes, and nothing is ever simple. Experienced players confidently fire in devious shots that they've played a thousand times before, to place the ball inches from the hole. When an incredible 'ace' is sunk, they tend to let you know about it, which can be very 'off-putting' for those close by.

Holes 5 and 12 are considered to be two of the more challenging on the course, cruelly designed with the hole position in the middle of a small mound, and failure to place the ball on the mound, or preferably in the hole first time, will see it slide away to one side. Players then attempt to hit the ball back up the slope, hoping to judge the angle and speed perfectly, but the ball excruciatingly circumvents the hole before dropping over the other side. Many overshoot repeatedly as they move back and forth, with increasingly furrowed brows, until they collect the maximum number of shots (seven) and have to admit defeat. In two or three calamitous minutes, a player's expectation of glory can be devastatingly shattered.

The better players step up to the same dilemma, but are armed with a dishevelled notepad and often a selection of photographs which advise them of the exact shot to make wherever the ball stops. Don't be surprised to see the notepad come out more as the tension turns up a few notches.

At the end of every round, competitors hover around the officials who quickly post up a leader-board of the current positions, offering a glance at how far ahead, or behind, the players are. Both courses have eighteen holes, and a good score is anything around 40. Championship-winning standard is a score below 36, while over 55 and you can stop thinking about a podium finish.

Scores are cumulative, and after 108 holes the top eighteen players contest a final round of crazy golf to determine who will become World Champion. Unlike the previous six rounds, each group of players take turns with their shots, rather than holing out before the next player putts, which gives an advantage to those with croquet experience. This twist to the proceedings allows the opportunity for some minor aggression, as competitors can knock their opponent's ball out of the way.

HISTORY

Inspired by an idea between friends, the World Championship began in 2003 with a very international feel, attracting leading contenders from Finland and Tibet. Tim Davies won the first four contests, but was finally ousted in 2007. There is also a young female prodigy from the Czech Republic, with father in tow, who regularly competes for the title. At the tender age of eight in 2003, Olivia Prokopova managed to finish third overall – however, having a golf course in the back garden does help. She also holds the course record of 32 for the mini-golf, a score that wouldn't get the less talented halfway round. Incidentally, the record for the crazy golf is 31, but Olivia doesn't hold that record ... yet.

ESSENTIALS

This is a hugely popular event, with places often taken up months beforehand – the top eighteen players from the previous year have a place guaranteed. Joining the British Mini Golf Association (BMGA) will improve chances of entry, and thereafter it's on a first-come basis. All competitors must also check in before a set time, usually 9.30am, on both days to secure their place.

There's free practice between 9.30am and 9pm on the Friday, and outside the contest hours over the weekend. There are generous cash prizes for the top players, trophies for the top females and further prizes for best fancy dress and most abysmal performer ... something for everyone 'not' to aim for.

There are about 28 Championship rules in force over the weekend, and beginners should make themselves familiar with most of them. They should especially be aware of the repositioning rule whereby, if an obstacle restricts the movement of the club (e.g. a wall, water), the ball can be repositioned, but by no more than eight inches without incurring a penalty shot (expect much bending of this rule as players add on an extra inch or so to get closer to the hole). Should the ball land in a water hazard, you can either take a penalty or attempt to play it ... just don't get your feet wet. Beginners may want to bring along a pair of wellies!

There are hundreds of balls available in crazy golf, but for the World Championships only official balls may be used. The best players use 'professional putters', which are much heavier than standard ones and have a rubber face attached to the head (presumably this is to cushion the blow when competitors

attack each other to relieve the tension). These differences allow for better ball control, which is essential in crazy golf. Ordinary golf putters are fine too, but if possible avoid wooden mallets (see above) and improvised camera tripods!

TIPS

Each hole has its own nuances, from divots in the turf to various angles. Add wind direction, rain and a few big waves, and each hole becomes a conundrum. The obvious tip is to practise on the course, which is just what the top players do, and even they usually manage at least one poor round, so don't throw in the towel too soon. It's better to aim for a two-putt every time, placing the ball just short of the hole, rather than going for a hasty hole-in-one. During windy conditions, prevent unwanted roll of the ball by sheltering it with your body or by placing a marker underneath. There's nothing worse than seeing a first shot creep close to the hole, only for a gust of wind to suddenly drag it back behind the start line!

As for attire, this is not a typical golf course. The only plus-fours you'll see will be on beginners' scorecards. Whatever you wear, don't follow the example set by the caped crusaders, Batman and Robin, who found it impossible to play shots with the cape blocking their view of the ball. Finally, for the truly pretentious, bring along your golf trolley and caddie!

In the words of Tim 'Aceman' Davies, ex-World Champion: 'You win with ability, confidence, experience, manfulness, acumen and being a complete nutter. But the more I practise, the luckier I get!'

(**WACKY FACT**)

Tim Davies has co-written a must-read book (and DVD) called *Nutters with Putters*. Putting technique, stance and strategy are all discussed, alongside Championship-winning psychology and the all-important mind games necessary to unnerve your opponent.

IF YOU LIKE THIS

Become a member of the BMGA and play in various tournaments all year round. There are many other recognised mini-golf courses dotted around the country, from Dawlish to Southend, which can offer much-needed practice (see www.miniaturegolfer.com). For an even crazier slant on golf, try Disc (Frisbee) Golf, which doesn't require a ball or a putter! Players must instead throw a disc towards a metal basket, using as few attempts as possible – unfortunately there are no clubs for angry competitors to chuck in the air in disgust when a shot goes awry!

WORLD WALKING THE PLANK CHAMPIONSHIPS

'Ahoy, me hearties!'

Location: Queenborough, Isle of Sheppey, Kent

Date: A Sunday in August

Time: Afternoon (at high tide)

Entry fee: £5 (proceeds to charity)

Further information:
www.captaincutlass.com

Grid reference: TQ 908 722

Spectator Fun: ★★★

Wackiness: ★★★

World Champion: ★★★

Pain Factor: ★★

Training Required: ★★★

Family Friendly: ★★★★

WHAT HAPPENS

The *Salty Sea Pig*, a pirate ship moored in Queenborough harbour, is the venue for one of the more bizarre contests of the year as 'landlubbers' walk the plank to stand a chance of winning the £100 prize.

Walking the plank is a method of torture where victims are made to walk off an extended beam on the side of a ship, usually blindfolded and with hands tied. Drowning is the usual cause of demise, unless the sharks get to them first. Luckily, the waters off the Isle of Sheppey aren't believed to be shark-infested, but the crew of the *Salty Sea Pig* are just as ruthless as they were in the 18th century when plank walking was first believed to have been practised.

Unlike other events where speed, strength or accuracy contribute to success, here it's all about performing to the crowd, and the better an exhibitionist you are, the more chance you have of winning.

Entrants, some grudgingly encouraged, are rowed across to the *Salty Sea Pig*, with the motley crew on board casting evil stares. After a brief interrogation by the compere, the competitor engages in some bilge-sucking with Captain Cutlass (that's insults, for the landlubbers among you), drawing heavily on piratical language such as 'Avast ye swabs', or 'Ah'll give ye a taste o' the cap'n's daughter'. Piratical talk is one of four disciplines that judges consider when scoring the jumps. Once the verbal battle is over, there's a mini one-sided duel or some mock swashbuckling before the contestant is inevitably lured to the end of the plank.

With no escape, they take the plunge with the intention of impressing the crowd. There are three judges, and besides

good use of the pirate lexicon, they will award points based on costume, style of jump (including amount of splash) and any other improvisations that are delivered.

There are two types of contestant. Some plankers forgo fancy dress and role-play, throwing themselves into the water with very little assistance from Captain Cutlass. Then there are the serious entrants who see the event as an opportunity to reveal their true exhibitionist side. There are memorable performances each year from Heini Nielsen, the back-flipping Dane, dressed in sheepskin loincloth and sporting a viking hat, and Mad Mike, twice winner who entered one year with his rocket-propelled space hopper, even setting fire to his hair and bike. Other past entrants have included a nun with a dummy and a member of the Monster Raving Loony Party, who cycled off the plank.

No grog and gruel for the winners: instead they receive a very nice shield and £100-worth of gold doubloons – though the winner will need to keep an eye out for the scurvy crew of the *Salty Sea Pig* who may want their booty back.

HISTORY

First held in 1997 as a publicity stunt to raise the profile of the Isle of Sheppey. The organisers originally thought about cannon ball throwing, but deemed it too dangerous! The first few years were plagued with mishaps, including the dilemma of how to run the contest without a boat. Organisers decided to tie a makeshift plank to the end of a jetty, but unfortunately they failed to consider very heavy contestants and a 22-stone woman managed to break the plank. The following year, officials parked a car on top of the plank to prevent a similar disaster. Another time, officials realised at the very last minute that they had no plank for the contest, requiring a mad dash to the builders' merchants.

Even introducing a floating pontoon didn't end the problems, as the heavier competitors found themselves slowly sinking before they had a chance to walk. Luckily, there was a permanent solution in 2001 when officials borrowed a replica of Queen Victoria's royal yacht. In 2006, the *Salty Sea Pig* wasn't available, but organisers managed to bring in its sister ship, *Edith* … not exactly a name conjuring up images of throat-cutting pirates.

Former champion Long John Lenton declared one year that he would release a giant parrot and a large number of helium balloons into the sky as he jumped off, but the Civil Aviation Authority refused to allow this because the contest takes place under the flight path to Heathrow. When he reluctantly toned down his entry, the parrot failed to fly anyway!

ESSENTIALS

Entry is on the day, on a first-come basis, with a minimum age of eighteen. For obvious reasons, all entrants must be able to swim, but there is a safety crew in the water. Both men and women can enter, but the latter have to be encouraged more by the boisterous crowd to walk the plank. There is a limit of one hour for the contest, which is the time that the harbour is deep enough, and around 30 jumpers normally make the walk.

TIPS

Be original. If you come dressed as a pirate with a fluffy parrot and jump off the plank you won't win, so increase your chances by exhibiting plenty of imagination. One contestant vaulted off the plank with an inflatable shark and proceeded to stage a fight in the water, gaining maximum points for improvisation.

Study the piratical language and learn a few good phrases … just don't accuse Captain Cutlass of being 'a son of a biscuit eater' or he'll cut you up first! Finally, always use the wrong part of the verb, e.g. 'I be' or 'you be', and begin each sentence in a deep, throaty voice. For extra practice, 19 September is known as International Talk Like a Pirate

Day (www.talklikeapirate.com) and offers the perfect opportunity to sharpen up your pirate banter.

WACKY FACT

Before competitors walk the plank, Captain Cutlass is obliged to remind them all, for insurance reasons, that there is a risk of getting wet. Bizarrely, everyone is asked if they can swim and whether they accept liability for their clothes. What next ... whether they have a problem with sharks?

IF YOU LIKE THIS

Enter the Bognor Birdman (see page 128) for a much bigger splash, where entrants voluntarily jump off the end of the pier in a variety of ludicrous costumes.

NEWTOWN SANTA RACE

'Hundreds of Santa Clauses limber up for a gruelling road race. Let's hope they don't bring the reindeer!'

Location:	Newtown, Powys
Date:	A Sunday in December
Time:	11am
Entry fee:	£10 (plus sponsorship)
Further information:	www.santarun.info; Dial a Ride, 01686 622566
Grid reference:	SO 108 916

Spectator Fun:	★★
Wackiness:	★
Pain Factor:	★
Training Required:	★★★
Family Friendly:	★★★★

WHAT HAPPENS

Beards, big bellies and a hearty roar are all pre-requisites in this 4.5-mile, sartorially challenging, road-running race, which has even broken a world record. Fortunately for the entrants, there are no chimneys on the course!

Hundreds of competitors line up to become the fastest Santa, as the town becomes awash in a sea of red and white. Besides the serious athletes and not-so-competitive fun runners, wheelchairs, prams and even dogs take part, although the canine 'Santa Claws' have some difficulty keeping their beards on.

The main race begins in the high street with two giant inflatable Santa Clauses marking out the start line. Prior to the send-off, competitors are put through their paces with an impromptu aerobics routine, although stretching and jumping

up and down is probably asking too much for most people, who struggle to keep various festive appendages attached.

Severely underweight Santas straddle the start line, with baggy outfits, sawn-off trousers, padded bellies and trainers replacing the customary black boots. Towards the back lurk the more genuine contenders for the real Father Christmas. Moments to go, and competitors have one last tug of the belt and a 'Ho ho ho' before the off. As everyone heads through town, the younger children in the crowd wipe their eyes in disbelief, realising a big flaw in the Father Christmas story, and posing awkward questions later on for their parents!

The race moves quickly out of the centre, with those keen to lighten the load leaving behind a trail of discarded beards and hats, while some, with waists more appropriate for one of Santa's elves, are in danger of losing their oversized pants too. The course heads past the football ground, providing an early opportunity for some food and drink for those keen to replenish lost calories, just in case their stomach begins to shrink. The leaders continue to run through the back streets until they reach the Flying Shuttle pub, which is also the halfway marker.

The runners then hit the main road for about half a mile, with regular adjustments to the costume and a quick itch. The route then winds its way alongside the river before doubling back towards town. Those who have partaken of a few drinks along the way will need to be careful not to stray too much from the path at this point: the Santa outfits are snowproof ... not waterproof!

The crowd line the course for the last 100 yards, offering Santa Clauses a chance to mock their own appearance with a sprint that would put Prancer to shame. The dishevelled-

looking leaders cross the finish line, their beards barely clinging on and their suits torn apart. Winning times are around
22 minutes for the men and 26 minutes for women. Back
down the course, the slower runners wish they had brought
along Rudolph and the sleigh for a quicker mode of transport to the finish line, but all eventually trudge home with
more red cheeks than noses on display, barely managing a
single 'ho'!

HISTORY

This unique fund-raising race was the brainchild of Dougie
Bancroft of the Dial-a-Ride charity, to fund an office move,
and despite initial difficulties it attracted 501 entrants for its
first run in 2001. The idea, as always, was an epiphany while
in a pub, and three years later a new Guinness World Record
was set for the 'largest gathering of Santas', when 4,260 competitors dressed up for the run in the necessary garb of red
suit, belt, hat and fake beard (real beards obviously don't
count!). The record would have been broken a year sooner
had it not been for a sudden Santa convention in Tipai.

Previously, the record belonged to Bralanda in Sweden
where 2,685 raced. Since then the mantle has passed on to
the bigger stages of Liverpool and Las Vegas (7,269 Santas is
the current record), and with Adelaide and Milan also now
competing, it's unlikely that the record will ever return to the
sleepy mid-Welsh town. Newtown have accepted defeat grace-
fully and even attempted other world records, including in
2005 when they decided to see how many yo-yoing Santas they
could get in one place (all shouting 'Yo yo yo', no doubt).

ESSENTIALS

Entries can be made from July onwards, allowing enough time for competitors to work on their belly and beard. All competitors receive a Santa suit which they can keep and re-use on Christmas Eve, provided they haven't lost it on the course. Registration on the day is from about 8am. The fastest male and female Santa Clauses receive a trophy (and probably invitations to deliver some presents), and all finishers get a medal, but no mince pies, sadly! There's no time limit to complete the course, with some known to take as long as six hours, but with fifteen pubs on the route, it's amazing that some runners make it back at all. The race, which raises funds for the elderly and immobile, has unsurprisingly been designed to be flat and wheelchair-friendly. There are usually three water stations along the route.

There's also a shorter race of around 600 yards for children, starting after the main race, in which all finishers, including those given a helping hand, are rewarded with a goody bag.

TIPS

Don't expect to turn up and win unless you are already a serious runner. 4.5 miles at the best of times can be demanding, even without a tight-fitting outfit and inclement December weather.

Competitors should also avoid wearing too many layers of clothing underneath the deceptively warm outfit. A pair of shorts and a T-shirt should be sufficient, unless you intend to treat the race as a leisurely walk. However, don't go too bare, otherwise you will find yourself itching all over as the outfit conflicts with sweating limbs.

WACKY FACT

In 2004, long after the race had finished and everyone had gone home, there was a festive street brawl involving a large number of misbehaving Santas, who had probably had far too many brandies with their mince pies. The red-faced Santas were nothing to do with the race earlier in the day, which always manages a family-friendly spirit. Incidentally, one of the policemen on the scene that day was PC Slaymaker!

IF YOU LIKE THIS

Barnstaple in North Devon hosts the Barum Santa Fun Run. Held at the football ground, the race has fewer competitors and a much shorter distance and will therefore appeal to those with a bigger appetite for mince pies than exercise. Besides Liverpool, which still boasts the biggest get-together of Santas in the UK, there are other races in Battersea Park, Glasgow and Leeds. Meanwhile, Pasto in Colombia attempted to break the world record for the largest gathering of Santas on bicycles in 2007. At this rate Rudolph will be out of a job!

COOPER'S HILL CHEESE ROLLING

'You don't need to be completely crackers to take part, but it helps!'

Location:	Cooper's Hill, near Brockworth, Gloucestershire. Off the A46 road between Cheltenham and Stroud
Date:	Spring Bank Holiday Monday
Time:	From midday
Entry fee:	None (donations only)
Further information:	www.cheese-rolling.co.uk
Grid reference:	SO 892 147

Spectator Fun:	★★★★★
Wackiness:	★★★★★
Pain Factor:	★★★★★
Training Required:	★
Family Friendly:	★

WHAT HAPPENS

The crème de la crème of the wacky events calendar, the Cooper's Hill Cheese Rolling is one of the oldest, and certainly one of the craziest races in the world.

If you get your kicks from throwing yourself off the top of a hill, with pointless if not sheer wanton abandonment, to chase a lump of cheese, then this event is for you. The ostensible aim is to be the first person to get hold of the cheese. However, nobody ever catches up with it in mid-race, in which it apparently reaches speeds of 70 mph (although sometimes the cheese does collide with a photographer, allowing the runners to temporarily overtake it).

The cheese in question is a Double Gloucester which weighs 7lb, and there are usually five races, including one for women only. The actual course varies in gradient (in places it's as steep as 1 in 1), and with an extremely uneven surface it's very difficult for competitors to remain upright.

Serious entrants sensibly choose football boots and straps for every bodily joint. They also probably have a stash of painkillers just in case things go pear-shaped. For the rest, fancy dress is the popular choice, with many competitors arriving in sumo wrestling suits and ironic costumes based on flying action superheroes (but some won't need any help from their costumes to take off!).

At the top of the hill, there's a lot of pushing and shoving as competitors vie for a chance to be the first on the hillside. Eventually a line-up is established, with experienced chasers making an annual pilgrimage alongside complete beginners, and together they create a gladiatorial appearance on the skyline as haunting figures cling to the edge, threatening an imminent attack on those below (moments later the bottom of the hill will resemble the aftermath of a fight in the Colosseum). Nervous mutterings of 'What the hell are we doing here?' and 'I don't even like cheese!' fly across the hilltop as the seconds tick down.

The Master of Ceremonies prepares the competitors with a teasingly slow count to three, before the guest roller dispatches the cheese downhill. On the command of 'And four to be off', the chasing pack race off at the double in pursuit of the cheese, and quite often the runners are so excited that there's a false start. Unfortunately, this is one event where a recall is impossible, with most runners already halfway down before anyone realises that the cheese is still at the top.

There's no turning back once the chase starts, as a near-vertical drop confronts competitors immediately. Out of the 30 or so who take part, only three or four actually go hell-for-leather after the cheese, all exhibiting an utter lack of

self-preservation. The majority of cheese chasers futilely attempt a more diligent chase, preferring to ride on their backsides (during wet conditions they have no option) and bouncing to the bottom with their body semi-intact, which isn't really in the nature of an event that deserves a kamikaze attitude. Nevertheless, there are plenty of entangled limbs as competitors collide even when they do their best to put the brakes on, and a few eventually break into a brief run on the safer and flatter lower section to satisfy themselves that they did try to chase the cheese.

The winner, after performing several unintended somer-saults and bounces, usually races uncontrollably over the fin-ish line in around ten seconds. A trail of flour demarcates where the end is, but competitors don't slow down until they hit the bales of hay at the bottom with a thud, clutching their ankles or backside in agony. Volunteers at the bottom try to

slow down the participants, but often end up being rugby-tackled to the floor themselves.

The winner receives the cheese that he or she has chased in vain, and regardless of how sore they are, they manage to hold the cheese aloft to the delighted crowd. Winners need to keep a firm hold of the cheese after the race – one unlucky former winner had his cheese stolen while receiving treatment for a broken arm. Small cash prizes are given for second and third, probably just enough to cover a taxi ride to Accident and Emergency! For the rest of the field it's a case of 'hard cheese', but all are happy enough to walk away in one piece.

HISTORY

Cheese rolling has been going on for hundreds of years, with possible roots in Roman times, or even having pagan origins. The tradition may also be associated with a ritual for protecting grazing rights. No one really knows. Originally held at midsummer, today it's a firm fixture on the Spring Bank Holiday. Competitors come from all over the world to participate, with spectators numbering in excess of 3,000.

The cheeses are hand-made by a local dairy farm, and they must find it hard to watch as their hard work tumbles down Cooper's Hill. The Double Gloucester is protected with cardboard and plastic tape to prevent it from disintegrating. However, during the rationing period of 1941 to 1954, organisers introduced a single wooden cheese and with permission from the government included a token piece of real cheese in the centre. Winners during this period had the double misfortune of walking back up the hill to return the cheese in time for the next race.

Local man Stephen Gyde has won a record 21 cheeses, including a hat-trick of cheeses in 1980 and 1991, which he achieved even though he had to climb the hill three times to enter each race! Other illustrious winners in the past have included Marc Ellis, a former All Blacks rugby player, and Padam Shreer, a Gurkha, who both won cheeses in 2004. In 2007, Japanese TV star Daisuki Miyazaw came second after performing several death-defying back-flips. Groaning in agony, he commented: 'We are strong, but it hurts so much!'[1]

---

[1] From www.mirror.co.uk

Unfortunately, due to the annual debate on the safety of competitors, rumours of a permanent cancellation regularly circulate, with an increasing number of spoilsports trying to end a long tradition of madness. Only around 25 injuries are self-inflicted each year, many superficial and due to inexperience, but broken limbs do occasionally happen.

ESSENTIALS

The races take place every twenty minutes and if you do wish to take part, allow plenty of time to ascend the hill to queue. The minimum age for the downhill races is eighteen. All entries are on the day and there are announcements for lunatics before each event. To guarantee a good viewing point, aim to reach the hill by 10am. For those with too much self-preservation, there are uphill races for children, men and women, but obviously without the cheese. Though physically demanding for the competitors, these are not very exciting for spectators, but there's sometimes the comical sight of a small child giving up halfway and then tumbling back down.

Getting to the hill involves a short but tricky climb up to Cooper's Hill via a very muddy path. Wear appropriate footwear, especially if the weather is on the wet side. Should you bring children or the elderly, it's safer to watch the races from the fields below Cooper's Hill rather than attempting to negotiate the walk up either side. Alongside the cheese rolling race, over-excited spectators often set off their own mini-version of the tradition, since one stumble on the slippery slope sends a group of people toppling over like a pile of dominoes.

The risks to spectators often come from the cheese itself. The path that the cheese follows is not pre-determined; it can go anywhere, at any time, and hit anyone! In 2006 the cheese ploughed into a section of the crowd. Once the cheese sets off, don't take your eyes off it. You have been warned!

The event itself requires much planning and organisers spend weeks beforehand clearing the hill of any scrub and putting in place the safety net for spectators. Everyone should respect the tradition and, because there is no official sponsorship, should contribute to the costs by using the official car parks. Search and Rescue Aid in Disaster teams provide first aid cover on the hill itself and are occasionally required to extricate children stranded halfway up. Their absence in 2003 (due to an earthquake in Algeria) meant the event could not go ahead. Nevertheless, organisers rolled a single cheese to keep the tradition going, and beforehand an unofficial cheese roll took place with a yellow ball. St John Ambulance are stationed at the bottom, ready for a roaring trade in injuried bodies.

TIPS

Do not enter unless you are experienced or stupid. Jason Crowther, winner on several occasions, typifies the latter, declaring at the end of one race: 'I heard something crack which I think was my knee, but you just go for it!'[2] It's recommended not to copy this tactic.

---

[2] From www.mirror.co.uk

If the temptation for bravado gets the better of you, treat the hill with some respect. For an injury-free chase, avoid other competitors and lean back as you find yourself almost descending on your backside. Those who attempt to 'run' downhill, especially in drier conditions, will almost certainly require medical attention, with common injuries including finger dislocations, nosebleeds and sprained ankles. Supportive clothing and footwear will minimise damage, but such precautions are not considered in the spirit of the tradition.

Finally, some advice from Steven Brain, winner of seventeen cheeses: 'The trick is to try to stay on your feet.' However, attempting his eighteenth cheese, Steven managed to break his ankle![3]

Potential entrants should pay heed to an announcement made several years ago, that perfectly sums up the madness of cheese rolling: 'The races will be delayed for a short while until the ambulances return.' You've all been warned!

WACKY FACT

The 1997 chases saw a record 33 injuries, most of them minor, but exaggerated safety concerns precipitated the event's cancellation the following year. However, traditionalists still rolled a solitary cheese early in the morning with a small number of locals in pursuit.

---

[3] From http://news.bbc.co.uk

IF YOU LIKE THIS

The Stilton Cheese Rolling offers cheese chasers a gentler contest, without the need to take out health insurance beforehand. Taking place on May Day Bank Holiday in Stilton, near Peterborough, Cambridgeshire, this is a team event where the competitors are able to keep up with the cheese.

There are races for men, women and children. In 2006, there was even a wheelchair race, including a team of basketball players. The cheese must only be rolled with the hand and cannot be picked up, kicked or thrown, which is slightly different to Cooper's Hill, where the cheese does exactly what it likes.

There is also cheese rolling at Ide Hill, Sevenoaks held on the Spring Bank Holiday Monday. Meanwhile, for a completely sedate cheese rolling tradition, head to the Randwick Wap in Gloucestershire, where three cheeses are pushed around the church and through the village of Randwick. The custom was originally a bequest to distribute food to locals, and is now carried out as part of the village festival. The following week, two of the cheeses are pushed down a nearby hill, but without the mayhem associated with Cooper's Hill. Watch out for the mop man!

WORLD EGG THROWING CHAMPIONSHIPS

'Have a cracking good time!'

Location: Thorpe Latimer Park, Swaton, near Sleaford, Lincolnshire. Between Helpringham and Swaton on the B1394

Date: A Sunday in late June (part of the Swaton Vintage Fair)

Time: From 1pm

Entry fee: Admission to fair (about £4 per adult) but free to enter the championship

Further information: www.eggthrowing.com

Grid reference: TF 132 397

Spectator Fun:	★★
Wackiness:	★★
World Champion:	★
Pain Factor:	★★
Training Required:	★★
Family Friendly:	★★★★

WHAT HAPPENS

An 'egg-centric' contest of throw and catch – just hope you don't end up with egg on your face!

Competed in pairs, the objective is to chuck a raw egg to your partner without breakage; the catch is that after each round, teams must move further apart until there's just one team left standing with an unbroken egg.

Teams enter the throwing arena wearing safety goggles and luminous orange raincoats with pointed hoods, and line up ten metres apart. With over twenty teams participating, somebody just turning up and seeing this could easily mistake the event for a bizarre ritual ... maybe the 'chuck-chuck clan'!

Eggs are thrown cautiously at first, with the catcher spreading their legs and cupping their hands, ready to gently

embrace the oncoming missile. At this early stage, splats are in short supply as the eggs are comfortably caught. After the first round, teams are shepherded further apart, around five metres, and with the increased distance comes a greater risk of smashes.

After several rounds, the breaking distance is reached for many of the competing teams, as the free-range eggs become out of range. The catcher eyes the launched egg and begins to move sideways, then forwards, before frantically back-ped-alling in a mad scramble – only for the missile to slip through their fingers, splattering over their face and chest. As if the contest wasn't difficult enough, sometimes a wayward throw requires the catcher to dive to their left or right in the faint hope of producing an epic save, but instead they collide into another competitor, before berating their partner.

Fortunate competitors inadvertently discover that even though the eggs fail to make the distance or find a safe pair of hands, they inexplicably bounce and then continue rolling intact, watched in disbelief by rivals who wonder whether they switched their eggs for the hard-boiled variety. Other teams blatantly copy the rolling technique rather than risk throwing the egg to their partner.

However, the purists stubbornly refuse to stoop that low, and continue to be loyal to the true essence of the contest as they stick to the chuck-and-catch method. Unless teams have practised a tried-and-tested technique, just sticking a hand out as the egg flies through the air will inevitably lead to a splat. Often, competitors lose their balance in a pathetic attempt to cushion the catch, suffering the double ignominy of falling over backwards while being splattered with egg. Losing teams are consoled with sympathetic crowd applause

as they are whisked away, leaving behind those teams that have turned the contest into an egg-rolling discipline.

As the distance increases, technique becomes redundant, and no matter what tactics teams adopt, success depends more on the strength of the egg, and if it can withstand any more abuse. Beyond 60 metres, the younger entrants especially find the target unreachable, but a further twist in the rules requires the egg only to roll past the halfway mark to count as a valid attempt. Eventually, the same distance decides the winner, with one egg breaking and the other bouncing. The winning team are required to smash their egg to prove there has been no 'fowl' play.

The 'egg-bouncing' champions will find it a lot harder to defend their title in future years – the organiser has promised to be more ruthless, and the word so far is that competitors will need to catch the egg in one piece, without bouncing, rolling or any other shenanigans that the more devious teams think up. Performance-enhancing aids are forbidden, and that includes the use of a baseball glove or fishing net.

HISTORY

The inaugural championship took place in 2006 and was won by a team of New Zealand turkey farmers, with a distance of 72 metres. They admitted afterwards that they practised with ostrich eggs back home. The championship is organised by the World Egg Throwing Federation, who actively protect the integrity of egg throwing throughout the world.

John Prescott, who was infamously hit by an egg during a visit to Rhyl in Wales, was invited to attend in 2006 but declared himself engaged for the foreseeable future. The Egg Throwing Federation even invited John to become their president, but like most politicians he clearly lacked a sense of humour and declined the post.

ESSENTIALS

The orange anoraks and goggles were provided for competitors in 2007 but you may want to bring along spare clothing, should you lose and end up with egg not just on your face. Don't forget to add some padding, lest the egg finds its way to a more delicate area of the body.

The whole day is an extravaganza of egg sports, also featuring the World Russian Egg Roulette Championship (see page 262) and an egg accuracy event, with one very reluctant volunteer bombarded by eggs all day. Scores are assigned to different parts of the body, with the more delicate nether regions receiving the higher score. The winner is whoever inflicts the most pain!

In total, over 1,000 eggs are broken throughout the day. But, before campaigners for the prevention of cruelty to eggs get too excited, the eggs used are free-range rejects of various odd shapes and sizes and all from happy homes. They also all comply with federation rules of a specific shell thickness and rawness.

TIPS

The key is to use both hands to catch the egg and to avoid over-clenching. It's advisable to catch the egg to the side of the body and, as it gets close, to bring the hands back slightly to reduce the impact. Whatever you do, don't catch one-handed or with the hands out in front. Under-arm throws are safer, but beyond a certain distance over-arm will be necessary.

Eggs tend to be more resistant on the edges than over the rounded middle part. It's therefore possible to minimise breakage if the egg is received by the catcher on either end … easier said than done.

WACKY FACT

The current World Egg Throwing record is held by Johnnie Dell Foley, who threw a fresh cackleberry to his cousin over an 'egg-ceptional' 98.51 metres in Texas in 1978. This is surely one egg record that will never be beaten!

(**IF YOU LIKE THIS**)

If the thought of a World Championship makes you nervous, enter the National Egg Throwing Championships in Tandridge, Surrey, which takes place every July in the more sedate surroundings of a village fete. If you can't throw an egg, maybe rolling is your forte – the World Egg Rolling Championship is held in Soar Mill Cove, near Salcombe, South Devon on Easter Sunday and there is also a famous egg rolling tradition in Preston, Lancashire (see page 323).

TETBURY WOOLSACK RACES

'A sackful of fun – just don't get caught napping!'

Location:	Gumstool Hill, Tetbury, Gloucestershire
Date:	Spring Bank Holiday Monday
Time:	From 2.30pm
Entry fee:	£5 per individual and £20 for a team

Further information:
www.tetburywoolsack.co.uk

Grid reference:	ST 891 931

Spectator Fun:	★★★
Wackiness:	★★
Pain Factor:	★★★★
Training Required:	★★★★
Family Friendly:	★★★★

WHAT HAPPENS

Gumstool Hill, where suspected witches were tormented in medieval times, has more recently become the location of a very challenging race to punish men, women and even children, leaving them all suffering from sheer exhaustion at the end.

Competitors race with a sack of wool that weighs 60lb (35lb for the women) up the notorious Gumstool Hill in Tetbury, starting near the Royal Oak at the bottom and finishing 240 yards later at The Crown. Entrants will need a stiff drink at the start to bolster confidence and, after surmounting the 1 in 4 gradient uphill, further beers to recover! The races are in heats, with the finals at the end of the afternoon.

Like lambs to the slaughter, competitors line up at the bottom of the hill. Looking up the course, the less-prepared entrants suddenly realise that they've had the proverbial wool pulled over their eyes after an ill-judged decision to accept a challenge from friends to enter a run-of-the-mill 'sack race'.

Before competitors even get going, they face the potentially embarrassing task of picking up the cumbersome woolsack. With an aggressive lift off the floor, they swing the sack onto their shoulders, trying not to knock themselves or other competitors over in the process. Tightly gripping the sack, they then run at full pelt, eager to strike into the lead and gain sufficient momentum in readiness for the uphill section. Left stranded at the start, there's always at least one entrant taking several clumsy attempts to haul the woolsack up before finally entering the race somewhat belatedly.

Within yards of the start, competitors hit the hill, with the very fittest bounding up and hardly breaking into a sweat, completing the entire race in under a minute. Standing with hands on waist at the finish line, they utter a few expletives without betraying any signs of fatigue, before heading off for a massage in preparation for the final.

The pace abruptly slows down to a near-standstill for the rest of the pack as the unforgiving hill leaves a painful first impression, although a combination of unabated enthusiasm and considerable crowd support pushes the competitors along the course.

Nearing the summit, competitors have the stuffing well and truly knocked out of them (unfortunately the sack remains stuffed), as head and shoulders slump into a very premature dip for the line. Those really struggling begin to suspect that a sheep remains attached to the wool, as the sack rams itself deeper into their back.

The weight of the woolsack and the rigours of the hill eventually take their toll on the competitors, now capable only of slow, wobbling strides.

The course stubbornly continues to climb, and the finish line remains below the horizon for what seems an age, tormenting and teasing the competitors as they mutter under their gasping breath, 'How much further!' The crowd, who have flocked to the steepest part of the hill to witness the more animated struggles, offer consoling ripostes which motivate competitors enough to step up a gear, until they develop a stitch and contemplate sacking it all in!

Reciprocated shouts of encouragement between flagging entrants help to keep the legs moving, but an intense rivalry returns as the finish banner comes into sight and competitors are keen to avoid last place. But any attempt at a short burst of pace only accelerates their fall over the line, as they dump the woolsack on the ground before literally hitting the sack. Many limp off straight to the pub, while others wish they had never put their name down for the relay races which soon follow!

The relay races involve teams of four running up and down the hill twice, with each member running one way only. Before anyone hastily volunteers to run one of the two 'easier' legs downhill, think again. Competitors find it surprisingly awkward and no less painful as they hurtle downhill, and those with a gangly appearance, or having had one too many beers, end up zigzagging menacingly towards the crowd, staggering under the unwieldy woolsack. After two or three abortive attempts to secure the woolsack on their back, they decide to rejoin the race with the sack hanging precariously over one shoulder, just about making it to the end without further calamity. They also decide there and then to run the easier, uphill leg next year!

HISTORY

The races probably date back to the 17th century, when young drovers at the town's thriving wool and yarn market drank too much ale and decided to exhibit their prowess to the local women by carrying a woolsack up Gumstool Hill. A modern version of the race has taken place since 1973, with the woolsacks provided by the British Wool Federation. The races are now the town's sole reminder of its wool heritage.

The course was originally 280 yards and run between the two pubs (which explains why the young drovers were so confident of their claims), but since 1999 the course has lost 40 yards, to the relief of those taking part. Current records for the men and women are 45.94 seconds and 1.05.69 minutes respectively, times that would be respectable running downhill without the woolsack.

The tough nature of the race has in the past attracted a team from the Royal Gurkha Rifles (without the rifles), some Australian sheep-shearers, and even one competitor attired in army costume complete with gas mask, who nevertheless still managed an impressive time.

The races have also had their fair share of 'sad sack' competitors, including the Norfolk Mountain Rescue team, a carrot promoting organic vegetables, and the Right Herbert, who every year attempts the course while pedalling a unicycle and carrying the woolsack. He succeeds in making a mockery of the main contest, effortlessly coasting along with only a slight wobble towards the end.

ESSENTIALS

The local sports teams make up the majority of entrants, alongside those who spontaneously give in to some bravado. There's prize money of £100 for both individual winners, while relay teams of four must share £200. Even the children get a chance to race, but with two concessions. They have the less arduous load of a stuffed pillowcase, and run in teams of four, with each racing only a quarter length of the course, although there's plenty of sympathy for the children assigned the leg running up the main hill.

The main street is always busy, so arrive early to gain a good vantage point on the hill, where you will be able see the start and finish as well as the gruelling middle section. The Woolsack Races are the highlight of Tetbury Woolsack Day, which also has a street fair, a charity auction, and street entertainment including jugglers and Morris dancers – but don't worry, watching the latter is not compulsory.

TIPS

Officials recommend that any potential competitors walk the course prior to entering. Strong legs and a very fit body are pre-requisites, with the more competitive-minded entrants advised to train with a sack of potatoes up and down a flight of stairs for a few weeks beforehand. It's crucial that competitors begin the race with the woolsack comfortably resting on the back of their head and shoulders, keeping a firm grip on the two front corners. Any other posture is likely to cause injury or a premature withdrawal. Unlike the old days, avoid drinking beer until after the race if you want to impress the spectators.

WACKY FACT

Gumstool Hill is named after the stool used in medieval times to dunk suspected witches. The stool was located at the bottom of the hill, but perhaps it should reappear and serve as punishment for those competitors not pulling their weight!

IF YOU LIKE THIS

For a completely different sort of handicap, head to Hereford Racecourse for a Wife Carrying Contest, preferably with the permission of your wife or another husband first. The idea for the 80-metre race has its origins in Finland over 100 years ago, when wife-stealing was common practice. Nowadays it's all about piggybacks and fireman's lifts and not upsetting your loved one as she dangles inches off the ground. The event takes place every autumn as part of a beer and cider day, and the winning husband receives the wife's weight in cider, but don't get too greedy when choosing your partner or you'll never finish the race.

For those with an appetite for extra wackiness, the famous Cooper's Hill Cheese Rolling takes place in nearby Brockworth earlier in the day. Both events are contestable without breaking the speed limit in between, but the Woolsack Races may be a hill too far for some.

WORLD POOH STICKS CHAMPIONSHIPS

'Where's Winnie-the-Pooh when you need him?'

Location:	Days Lock, Little Wittenham, Oxfordshire
Date:	A Sunday in March
Time:	From Midday
Entry fee:	£1.50 per Pooh stick
Further information:	www.pooh-sticks.com
Grid reference:	SU 566 934

Spectator Fun:	★★
Wackiness:	★★
World Champion:	★★
Pain Factor:	★
Training Required:	★
Family Friendly:	★★★★★

WHAT HAPPENS

A World Championship invented by a bear with a 'very little brain'! In the spirit of Winnie-the-Pooh, individuals and teams race short twigs, aka Pooh sticks (no need to hold your nose!), over a distance of roughly twenty metres ... just don't fall in the river.

The racing takes place on two bridges over the River Thames, before it gets too big, in the village of Little Wittenham. Competitors are provided with different-coloured Pooh sticks, each one about twelve inches long. Unfortunately, there's no opportunity to study the river before deciding on where best to drop the stick; instead, every colour has its own designated spot on the bridge, which leaves the races purely down to chance.

Each race consists of six competitors who, on the count of three from the eagle-eyed officials, drop their sticks into the river about twenty feet below – ideally without first colliding with the bridge and losing precious seconds. Competitors are not supposed to hurl or throw their stick to gain an advantage. This doesn't prevent some over-eager children and adults from applying a bit of force, provided they can avoid the scrutiny of the officials or the parents of the younger, law-abiding competitors – although the younger the competitor, the less strict the rules seem to be!

Once the sticks are safely in the water and floating downstream, competitors race to the other side of the bridge and poke their heads through or over the rails, hopefully catching a glimpse of their stick sailing through to the other side ... or maybe they'll see Eeyore float under! Unlike in the Winnie-the-Pooh books, where the first stick to appear from

under the bridge wins, here the stick must travel a little further downstream to sail under a rope finishing line. There's plenty of futile cheering, but whether it wins or not is all down to chance, depending on where the stick lies in the river.

The sticks bear left or right as they weave their way in and out of the currents, with one or two making the most headway and the rest taking their own good time to get to the finish. The odd sticky ending for competitors sees their Pooh stick grounded in mud or tangled up in reeds – definitely not a game for 'stick in the muds'. Often, one solitary stick will stubbornly refuse to appear from underneath the bridge, leaving the grown-up on the verge of a tantrum, though eliciting a smug grin from an eight-year-old boy alongside, whose stick sailed across the line in first place. Eventually the stick will reveal itself precariously close to the bank, to relieved

cheers, but too late for a comeback, and the competitor must bear up to defeat.

Motor boats regularly interrupt the races, creating plenty of swell in the river and making it more interesting for those in the next race. Each heat lasts two or three minutes, with the winner progressing through the knockout rounds until the grand final, usually involving more children than adults, plus the odd bear sneaking in too!

HISTORY

A local lock-keeper got the idea for the Pooh Sticks after watching people racing their own sticks off the bridge. Christmas time was the original date for the contest, but because of frequent icing over of the river, the event moved to March, much to the relief of the spectators. There's also a team event, with competitors coming from all over the world, many often finishing in the top three. In recent years, participants have travelled from Latvia, Australia and Japan just so they can throw sticks off a bridge!

The Pooh Sticks game itself first appeared in the Winnie-the-Pooh books, and it's believed that the original site was Poohsticks Bridge in Ashdown Forest, East Sussex, where A.A. Milne played with his son. But, unlike the World Championships, Winnie-the-Pooh and friends raced fir cones down the river, before changing to the more aerodynamic sticks, which they could easily mark.

The 2008 contest was the last year that the Rotary Club ran the event, when it also celebrated its silver anniversary. Hopefully 2009 will see the beginning of another 25 years of Pooh Sticks.

ESSENTIALS

This is a family event, not surprisingly, as it often falls on Mothering Sunday. Unlike other wacky contests, cheating is definitely not the done thing ... unless of course you're a child! Over 2,000 people enter the event, which means that the contest doesn't finish until the late afternoon – and expect lengthy queues in the earlier knockout rounds. There are other attractions (including a teddy bear clinic) to keep children and adults occupied, but car parking close by is limited to the disabled, so expect at least a half-mile walk. For anyone worried about polluting the river, volunteers from Wantage Diving Club fish out the sticks at the end; otherwise they would all drift downstream towards London, where bemused tourists at Tower Bridge would see thousands of coloured sticks float under it a week later!

(TIPS)

Enter only if you're under twelve years old! Luck definitely plays a major part in the contest, and fortunately for the organisers, who award a Winnie-the-Pooh teddy bear for the main prize, the more successful entrants tend to be the children – or is it just that adults concede their go before there's a flood of tears from one very unhappy competitor?

The essence of the event is perfectly described by Charles Cumming, captain of the winning team in 2008: 'The beauty of Pooh Sticks is that a five-year-old and a 90-year-old are evenly matched. There's no technique, no skill, no training. All you need are opposable thumbs!' There have even been runners-up as young as fourteen months … you've been warned! In the words of five-year-old Hannah Oakey, a former World Team Champion, 'the key is to believe in Winnie-the-Pooh'!

There is, however, some hope for the more competitive entrant who doesn't want to leave everything to chance. Consider where the river seems to be flowing quickest, or study which colour is most successful, before choosing your Pooh stick from the official. Another former World Champion recommends that you 'drop the stick horizontally so that it doesn't bounce back up when hitting the water, and it lands ready to float'. Also, 'try to get away with dropping on the count of two, not three' – but this tip is only for the smaller kids to try!

Of course, the surefire way for success is to bear in mind the advice handed out to Tigger from Eeyore, the real expert, by 'letting your stick drop in a twitchy sort of way, if you understand what I mean'.[1]

IF YOU LIKE THIS

For more childish pursuits, try the British Open Crabbing Championships, held in Walberswick in Suffolk every August. Children – and adults – have 90 minutes to find the heaviest crab using a single line and bait. The more cunning entrants bring along their own secret bait to entice the crab. Not sure what Eeyore would have made of this, though ... probably sounds like too much twitching!

---

[1] From *Winnie-the-Pooh*, by A.A. Milne.

WORLD'S GREATEST LIAR

'Not for anyone averse to bare-faced cheeks!'

Location:	Ye Olde Trip to Jerusalem pub, near Nottingham Castle, Nottingham
Date:	A Thursday in late November
Time:	From 8pm until late
Entry fee:	£3 to watch, no entry fee
Further information:	Ye Olde Trip to Jerusalem, www.triptojerusalem.com
Grid reference:	SK 570 394

Spectator Fun:	★★
Wackiness:	★★
World Champion:	★★★★
Pain Factor:	★
Training Required:	★★★★
Family Friendly:	★

WHAT HAPPENS

An evening of very tall tales, taking place in the oldest pub in the UK, so they say! Male competitors should avoid bringing along their wives, who will instantly spot if they are telling a lie or not.

About 60 people, plus a few gatecrashing ghosts, cram like sardines into the dingy Rock Lounge. As a taster for what lies ahead, organisers remind those competing that they stand a chance of winning the first prize of £12,500, but are quick to correct themselves before anyone in the audience falls for the first fib of the night. The winner actually receives a meal for two, which is probably a packet of pork scratchings!

The contest is organised by the local storytelling club, who obviously have an unfair advantage over newcomers. With the order decided randomly, the first entrant, having drawn the short straw, clambers over chairs and tables to find just enough space to stand up and begin their entry. Historically, those who speak in the first half of the evening have less chance of success since the audience, who decide the winner, drink enough beer to obliterate any memory of what happened earlier on.

Having recovered his breath from negotiating the obstacle course, the first contestant, a former World Champion no less, dives straight into an intriguing story about the world's first greatest liar, a man named Ezekiel Cooper, Nottingham's liar-in-chief, and his amazing half-price medicine, Cooper's Invigorating Larrup. The story twists and rambles seamlessly on with much aplomb, mentioning unemployed train drivers back in the 19th century, a family from hell, and how eventually Ezekiel's quack medicine was discovered to be nothing more than a concoction of cow's urine and river water (now served in the pub as their guest ale). After ten incredulous minutes, the audience are left gobsmacked and wonder whether they've just listened to a credible history lesson or a really good shaggy dog story.

The evening meanders on to tales of demonic possession in German motor cars, with frowns from the purist liars when the entrant incorporates props in the form of car symbols into the story. Then it's on to a sultan with 300 wives whose eunuch laboriously ferried each wife to his bedroom. The punchline – 'It's not the sex that kills you … it's the running after it' – produced many laughs, although was this a lie or a very bad joke?

Further tales of penguins, ghosts and mackerel dazzle the audience into a state of confusion. At the end, everyone in the room digs into the depths of their memory to vote for the greatest liar of them all, with the top three read out in reverse order. The winner accepts the accolade, but with the nagging thought that maybe the audience were also lying when they voted!

HISTORY

First held in 2000 with plenty of yarn spun since, and past winners have included an ex-superintendent of the police! A few years ago the organiser, Pete Davies, received a phone call at 5am from an Israeli radio station asking why they were offering a trip to Jerusalem as a prize for the winner. It didn't take long for Pete to put them right on that one, reminding the caller of the name of the venue where the contest was held.

The pub itself goes back to the 11th century, with more sordid history than you can fit into an entry in the contest, including tales of treason and ghosts, its own network of caves and even an old cockfighting pit. The venue for the contest houses a cursed model of a galleon, apparently causing death to those who touch it, but fortunately now sealed within a glass case. Worryingly for the younger females in the audience, there's also a pregnancy chair ... just ask which one it is before you sit down, or you may need to conjure up a whopper of your own to explain things to your boyfriend!

ESSENTIALS

The competition has just a few rules: no politicians, lawyers or double-glazing salesmen, although bizarrely there are no protests when professional storytellers enter! Competitors are not allowed to read from scripts, and although props are tolerated, regulars will also effortlessly whip out a lie with no assistance. Unless it has a specific purpose in the story, refrain from excessive use of expletives. The entry itself should be around ten minutes long; any longer and the audience will lie down for a kip.

Entry is on the night, with additional participants accepted during the contest. However, the venue is very small and an early arrival is essential to guarantee a seat, otherwise the organisers will lock you out. Officials dish out fines to anyone whose mobile phone rings during the contest ... and this is no fib. Food and drink is served in the public house throughout the contest – unfortunately the landlord isn't part of the contest when he hands you the bill!

The storytellers' website, www.storytellersofnottingham.co.uk, has essential advice for potential newcomers to the contest.

───────────────(TIPS)───────────────

There are several things to consider when putting together the lie. Firstly, it has to be plausible enough to convince the audience that it could just be true. The story should be delivered with a persuasive eloquence, ideally ending on an amusing punchline, even taking a well-known phrase and turning it around. The art to storytelling is to disguise any mistakes, either weaving back in the missed line or simply moving on – the audience will have no idea (especially after a few pints of beer). Involving the audience in the story will improve your prospects, and if you end up being picked to go near the end, avoid drinking too much of the local brew – it will not bode well if the story is punctuated with hesitations, stutters, copious 'umms' and 'errrs', or complete inarticulateness.

As for the story, professionals recommend working on the ending first, then going backwards. In the words of 2004 World Champion Pete Davies, a Greatest Liar needs to bear in mind the following words of wisdom: 'Don't lie, tell your story with a straight face and an angelic smile, and even if the crowd jeer and mock you, don't give in. The most successful lies have a lot of comedy in them and this is because the crowd find a laugh memorable. Anything too serious they don't enjoy because they know the score and what they want is utter cobblers, not smart plots.'

WACKY FACT

Regulars to the event proudly admit to having a repertoire of over 100 stories ... without the use of a script. Many stories are told off the cuff – just don't encourage them to reel off their back catalogue, or you may be there all night!

IF YOU LIKE THIS

Besides other storytelling nights, including spooky ghost tales, the organisers also hold a spoof séance involving a Viking called Nogwyn. Nogwyn is their spirit guide, contacted via an old Viking's helmet, authentically dated to the year 299 on a price label, and discovered in a bargain joke shop. The pub also hosts a Ringing the Bull Contest where competitors are required to swing a bull's metal nose-ring, hanging on a piece of string off the ceiling, onto a metal hook on the wall ... or is this just another load of bull?

The Bridge Inn in Santon Bridge, Cumbria is the venue for the World's Biggest Liar Contest, held every year and with a similar format to the Greatest Liar. The contest takes place in honour of former publican and legendary pork-pie-teller, Will Ritson, who relished pulling the wool over the eyes of the tweed-wearing climbers who frequented his pub. More recently, the entries have poked fun at the local communities, with tales of ram-raiding sheep and muttons of mass destruction. There was a first in 2006, when the contest was won by a woman. Fortunately, the winning entry, weaving in a tale of flatulent sheep (sheep anecdotes tend to impress the judges), was told by comedienne Sue Perkins, and garnered enough laughs to stave off a revolt from the locals.

One wonders which of the World Champion Liars is best: the Greatest or the Biggest?

THREE HORSESHOES WHEELIE BIN RACE

'Have a wheelie good time!'

Location: The Three Horseshoes pub, Staplestreet, Hernhill, near Faversham, Kent

Date: A Saturday in mid-July

Time: 1.30pm

Entry fee: £10 per team

Further information: The Three Horseshoes, 01227 750842

Grid reference: TR 059 601

Spectator Fun: ★★

Wackiness: ★★

Pain Factor: ★

Training Required: ★

Family Friendly: ★★★★

WHAT HAPPENS

There's no chance of taking out the rubbish as wheelie bins are recycled into colourful and crazy racing machines.

Teams of four, some of whom deserve to be in the loony bin, race over a short circuit (about 400 metres, but it will feel a lot longer) from The Three Horseshoes pub to Mount Ephraim Gardens and then back to the pub. One member of the team must climb inside the wheelie bin, wearing head protection just in case the bin tips over, and the essential nose peg should the team forget to empty the trash beforehand! The remaining three members are responsible for pushing or pulling the wheelie bin along the course. There's also one major change to the wheelie bin design, requiring

© The Three Horseshoes

all entries to have at least four wheels in contact with the ground at all times.

Streamlined wheelie bins that could grace any racetrack line up at the start alongside highly imaginative and flamboyant entries. For the latter, several glances are required to work out which part of the design is the original wheelie bin, and officials scrutinise the entries, ensuring there are no engines or pedal bins attached for extra propulsion. There are three drinks stations along the way, and each team member must take one half-pint of beer or lager at each of the stops. Teams will receive a five-second penalty for each beer not fully drunk ... fat chance of that happening!

Three wheelie bins at a time tackle the course, all competing against the clock. Every person in the team must have a turn in the bin, which precludes any tactical selections such as choosing three muscle-bound beer drinkers and a dainty young lady as passenger! With one competitor firmly wedged inside the receptacle with a couple of strategically placed airfresheners, and wondering how they'll ever get out again, the first teams waste no time in charging down the road.

The quicker teams flawlessly tip the beers down at each drinks station, remaining vigilant for any dustbin lorries passing through the village inadvertently mistaking their sparsely decorated bins for refuse collection, before hurtling towards the halfway point, and the horticultural splendour of Mount Ephraim.

Slower teams approach the short course as a full afternoon of entertainment, with absolutely no intention of racing, and refusing to rush their drinks – penalties would perhaps be more appropriate for teams who drink too slowly! Clumsy changeovers send competitors haphazardly jumping head-first into

© The Three Horseshoes

the wheelie bin (see above), perhaps betraying a few too many beers earlier in the day.

Back on the course, there are shouts of 'What a load of rubbish' from the crowd, directed at teams not trying hard enough, while empty cans and sweet wrappers are cheekily tossed into the bins as they pass by – that'll teach them for going too slowly! Sadly, there are no bonus points for teams collecting rubbish off the street. Those racing in upright bins with just a couple of tin cans for decoration soon regret not spending more time building their bins, as their unwieldiness leads to a few nervous wobbles and near-topples.

After an excess of beers and too much sun, the last few teams struggle to surmount the climb back to the finish with plenty of huffing and puffing. The faster teams complete the course in about eight minutes, and one team has even managed it in five minutes, worryingly quick for the local bin men and women, who fear for their jobs! A few teams always take about two hours, although it's a miracle that some of the 'trashed' teams ever make it to the end!

HISTORY

This is the biggest Wheelie Bin Race in Britain, first run in 2000 and usually contested by around twenty teams. Mike Skipper, landlord of The Three Horseshoes, conceived the contest after dismissing prams and wheelbarrows as too run-of-the-mill, but faced reluctance to racing wheelie bins until he demonstrated the much safer four-wheeled prototype.

One of the more popular teams are the Bentley Boys, who first entered the race with their wheelie bin disguised as a Bentley car. Since then they have entered a Spitfire and a train ... maybe next time it will be a spaceship? Other comical entries have included tanks, Daleks and even a wheelie bin in the guise of the Jamaican bobsleigh team.

ESSENTIALS

There are three categories: fastest bin, best-dressed team, and best bin, but don't expect any team to take a clean sweep of all three prizes! Each entry requires at least four wheels, with the two original wheels belonging to the wheelie bin touching the ground and the extra wheels and axle usually positioned where the lid of the bin would have been, but there's free rein for teams to do whatever else they fancy, as long as the bin remains human-powered. All members of the team must be touching the bin as they cross the finishing line.

Teams can enter only with a second-hand wheelie bin, so local people need not stand guard over their own bins in the weeks beforehand. The local council usually supply the bins and have even entered their own team in previous years. The race is the highlight of an all-day party, raising money for charity, with live music and a barbeque. At least the officials will have no problem finding somewhere to put all the rubbish the next day, although they're left with an unusual predicament: where do worn-out wheelie bins go when they're thrown out?

TIPS

This is one event where tips should definitely be avoided! Teams need to ensure that the lightest member of the team is in the bin when the race hits the toughest part of the course, after the final beer stop and heading back uphill. The faster teams design their bins lengthways with a horizontal bar added to the back for a better grip of the contraption. Slower teams should practise their beer-drinking to make up time at the pit stops.

WACKY FACT

A bin designed as the *Titanic* (an ocean-going bin liner!) was yards from the finishing line when it inadvertently found itself in someone's garden. Flares were set off, and the team eventually appeared in lifejackets and rowed to the end.

IF YOU LIKE THIS

Swimbridge in North Devon holds a festive Wheelie Bin Race on Boxing Day. Unlike The Three Horseshoes race, the bins race in their purest form, with teams having to wriggle their way through leftover turkey and wrapping paper in order to sit inside. The teams of two soon regret that second helping of Christmas pudding as they race down an extremely steep hill, the passenger shutting his eyes in sheer terror and warning his partner not to dare let go. The teams complete a quick route around the village, including a short-cut through the graveyard. When the race is over, there's still the matter of the annual tug-of-war contest, amusingly located over the river.

WORLD PIE EATING CHAMPIONSHIP

'A pie is for life, not just for Christmas'

Location:	Harry's Bar, Wigan, Lancashire
Date:	Mid-December
Time:	Midday
Entry fee:	Free
Further information:	Harry's Bar, 01942 243279
Grid reference:	SD 581 055

Spectator Fun:	★★
Wackiness:	★★
World Champion:	★★★
Pain Factor:	★★
Training Required:	★★
Family Friendly:	★

WHAT HAPPENS

Gluttons for punishment bid to be the fastest scoffer in town, but expect the locals to have the advantage – people from Wigan are nicknamed the 'pie eaters'!

With a quick time expected, the start is all-important and competitors prepare for a fast draw at 'pie noon', as soon as the chef has given his final approval for the competition pies (there are strict rules on the size of the chunks of meat and potato) and the gravy has passed the legendary Hindley Green Slump Test (see Essentials on page 237).

Champing at the bit, the locals stare at the pies, wide-eyed and salivating, in anticipation of eating their second pie of the day after the customary one for breakfast. Meanwhile, mischievous pie-eating virgins and outsiders opt for serviettes, which have nothing to do with etiquette, but are rather a cunning technique to catch any pastry purposely dropped without catching the eye of the officials, who will dish out yellow and red cards if they suspect excessive crumbing. Competitors disregard all other table manners, as they aim to be the first to finish their pie.

With officials on hand to watch for any false starts (probably easier to see who didn't false-start), competitors whip the tin foil off the pie – not an easy feat in itself – before diving into the delicious pastry, revealing underneath a meat and potato delight. As soon as the first chunk hits the mouth, outsiders vehemently exclaim, 'Yuck, the pie's cold!', but despite the unpleasant surprise, contestants take less than 30 seconds to get through half the congealment. Warm pies would certainly slip down a lot easier, though, and there are desperate pleas among the strugglers for the officials to pop the pies back in the microwave, and muffled cries of 'Where's the brown sauce?'

Tucking into the second half of the pie, competitors begin to develop a pasty complexion as the cold, stodgy taste hits home, disproving the old adage, 'as nice as pie'. Luckily, the toilets are just a pie's throw away, as the threat of puking increases.

The gravy boat stands redundant in the middle of the table, competitors considering pouring to be a waste of precious seconds. The use of gravy also hinders rapid and clean eating, once the equally unappetising dark brown slime has submerged the pie. However, when the chips are down, the heavy, non-chewable pastry does eventually push one or two competitors past the limits of mastication, and they concede to some extra beef flavouring. A cold pie is challenge enough, but tepid gravy is just one test too far, and not surprisingly, the unwise decision to add gravy sees their World Championship bid 'meat' a sticky ending.

Big bites are the only sensible strategy for winning the contest, washed down with gulps of water and not stopping until the last morsel of food has been ingested. As the intensity of the eating increases, so do the dangers, and the less fortunate contestants may even succumb to the local affliction known as 'swallow-stall', where the throat is blocked with part of the pie, caused by overzealousness and a desire to end the ordeal as soon as possible. Only a fast-working lubricant will prevent a trip to casualty, although after relieving the choking with half the contents of the gravy boat, a hospital visit could still be required to sort out the severe stomach cramps.

With a 'never say pie' attitude, there's one last effort to shovel in the final piece of the pie while still negotiating with the previous mouthful. Without a lick of the lips in sight, the winner is declared in under a minute and a new world record is set, subject to exposing a pie-free mouth.

The first dead heat occurred in 2007, requiring a 'pie-off' between the winners, who were both less than impressed that they were expected to eat another pie without any respite. Or maybe they conspired to prolong the eating contest on purpose? Fortunately, the rematch was over within a staggering 35 seconds, and the winner, who appropriately enough works in a bakery, made mincemeat out of his opposition. His large frame, big gob and beer belly for once proved that size does matter when it comes to food contests. He paraded the trophy, looking very pie-faced and maybe thinking to himself that he couldn't face another pie until at least mid-afternoon. The runner-up looked much the worse for wear, but luckily there was no need for the meat wagon!

HISTORY

First contested in 1992, when two customers in Harry's Bar decided to challenge each other. Originally, the aim was to wolf down as many pies as possible in three minutes (the record was only seven pies, but they were quite big). However, in 2006, the Vegetarian Society jumped on the pie wagon, declaring the contest unhealthy and demanding that a vegetarian alternative be included. Consequently, organisers moved swiftly to change the rules to just one pie, causing outrage among the locals who had been accustomed to taking part in the contest for a free gourmet lunch. There was no sign of the anti-meat-eating lobby in 2007, much to the relief of the organisers who considered their presence to be a threat to the credibility of the contest.

The event turned into a man-versus-beast contest in 2007, when Charlie, a Bichon Frise, entered the contest after he inadvertently staked a claim for the World Championship crown. Charlie's owner was responsible for storing the pies overnight, but accidentally left the fridge door slightly open as he went off to investigate a pigeon stuck in his chimney. On his return he discovered that Charlie had an unknown talent for pie-eating when he caught him in the act of munching his way through ten of them (hopefully not the same ones used in the actual contest).

Charlie's entry was originally a publicity stunt in the hope of attracting suitable replacements, but he took part anyway in a bid to become the first canine World Champion. Sadly,

Charlie made a dog's dinner of his attempt, perhaps letting the occasion overawe him, despite having the unfair advantage of a lifelong diet of Pedigree Chum. Future contests will probably see protests from animal rights campaigners or, worse, maybe a delegation of vegan poodles wishing to enter!

Not even canine intrusions could explain the setback that befell the 2008 contest. The chef responsible for the competition pies inadvertently used imperial instead of metric measurements, resulting in a mouth-watering pie, twelve inches across and three and a half inches deep. Luckily, word didn't reach the locals – who would have been quick to swarm around the pub – but it did mean the chef had to work around the clock to make up extra pies, at the correct size ... to the relief of the entrants.

Wigan's affinity with pies and their pie-eating nickname apparently goes back to the General Strike in the 1920s, when locals ate humble pie and went back to work. Although, after the success of locals in the World Championships, could it be that Wiganers are simply born and bred to enjoy their pies?

ESSENTIALS

The pies are 12cm long and 3.5cm deep, with pieces of meat and potato no bigger than 1cm cubed, which is apparently the optimum size for speed eating, requiring minimal chewing and with a low likelihood of choking. There's an annual dilemma for the chef not to make the pies too crumbly, which encourages facial spillage, nor too runny, which assists the competitors, thereby ruining the contest's reputation.

It's not only the pie that requires absolute perfection. Before the contest begins, the pie-master performs the highly scientific 'Hindley Green Slump Test', ensuring the gravy has the optimum viscosity for serving alongside the meat pie. Gravy is poured from a height of exactly ten centimetres onto a plate for ten seconds before officials measure the spread. Five centimetres is considered ideal; anything more and the gravy will be too diluted and aid the contestants (apparently the gravy boat was wrapped in barbed wire one year to prevent any competitors from taking swigs), while less than five centimetres will challenge competitors to swallow a treacle-like gunk.

Arrive about one hour before the start to secure a spot in the competition (this is, after all, a free pie contest in the town of pie-eaters), and don't forget to order your favourite drink to accompany the pie. There are no restrictions on who can enter, but vegetarians should watch the contest from a safe distance, just in case the aroma of a meat and potato pie tempts them to join in the celebration of carnivorous gluttony.

---------------------------------(**TIPS**)---------------------------------

Swallowing large lumps of congealed meat and potato, or even dog food, will help competitors to acclimatise ... as long as you don't mind gaining a few pounds before the contest. A propensity for eating meat pies isn't always an advantage, and indeed the 2007 winner admitted he was 'not too keen on meat pies' – obviously not a local – and 'would rather have a good curry'. He also endorsed the use of water, but not too much, or it slows down the gourmandising. Unlike other eating contests, it seems that this one does favour the larger competitor. Past winners have included a weight-trainer and an Australian rugby player.

WACKY FACT

In 2005, there was uproar among local bakeries when the honour of making the competition pies went to a company near Bolton. The locals vented their anger by picketing the venue, one local man even withdrawing from the contest as a sign of protest, only to berate himself later that day for passing up the opportunity of a free pie.

IF YOU LIKE THIS

Head to the Birnam Highland Games in Scotland for the World Haggis Eating contest, which takes place 60 miles north of Edinburgh in August. Competitors must eat one haggis (and you thought meat pies tasted awful) as fast as they can. There's even a Kilt Dash for those with good-looking legs, hopefully taking place before the haggis eating!

FOOTBALL IN THE RIVER

*'Crazy football players in a crazy game
watched by crazy people'*
Neil Teague (match referee)

Location:	Bourton-on-the-Water, Gloucestershire
Date:	August Bank Holiday Monday
Time:	4pm
Entry fee:	None (spectators only)
Further information:	www.bourtonrovers.co.uk
Grid reference:	SP 168 206

Spectator Fun:	★★★★
Wackiness:	★★★
Family Friendly:	★★★★

---------------(**WHAT HAPPENS**)---------------

The ultimate example of flowing football, where most of the action takes place underwater in a maelstrom of boisterousness, but also expect plenty of 'chuting' and dribbling in the wettest football match in the world!

Two local teams set up a pitch in the River Windrush, which runs through the pretty Cotswold town of Bourton-on-the-Water, attracting many bemused glances from tourists. Players anchor the goals in front of one of two bridges, and early arguments ensue over where the centre circle should be.

The town's football club supplies both teams, who are determined by age, turning the game into a battle of the generations. Each side has one goalkeeper and five outfield players, who wear either red or white football kits, rather than opting more sensibly for wellington boots and an anorak. At least the players' wives won't have any dirty kit to clean at the end.

Thousands of people throng both sides of the river, many pre-empting the afternoon's buffoonery by bringing along umbrellas. A few spectators even roll up their trousers, braving the river to be closer to the action, while resident ducks and fish eschew the game for fear of being mistaken for the ball.

The chairman of the football club accepts the onerous task of refereeing the game, and as kick-off approaches, he suspiciously eyes the waterlogged pitch. Players then test the referee's patience with some splashing of the opposing team, and even of the referee himself, before he retaliates with a verbal warning and then launches the ball into the air for the kick-off.

There's a frenetic pace at the start, as players are keen to impress the crowd with their dribbling skills, testing the leaky defence of the opposition with a spate of shots on goal. Not surprisingly, a deft piece of footwork fails abysmally, amounting to nothing more than a huge splash, knocking the ball a mere few feet forward. Tackling is nigh-impossible, with legs blindly thrust in the river aimlessly kicking water, or perhaps getting a faint touch of the ball – but the only thing passed will be water after a few too many beers later on.

The match is only fifteen minutes each way, which is just as well for the players, who find it extremely tiring expending energy without much progress – and who subsequently drift in and out of the action.

Without the aid of underwater cameras, many fouls go unpunished. The referee freely admits that he makes the rules up as he goes along, but diving tactics are definitely not

advisable. Anything else goes, with injuries usually self-sustained after players fall into the river that barely reaches their knees.

Teams even attempt a spot of water polo through frustration before the referee spots the handball and finally loses his temper, awarding the first of many yellow cards dished out over the course of the game. It's even been known for the odd red card to be handed out, but players won't know what not to do until the referee decides himself!

The referee has his hands full as the players surround him, clamouring for a penalty when a foul is committed close to the goal. Unfortunately, the white lines painted by the groundsman earlier in the day have since washed away and the referee has to wave away the protest, with the crowd shouting, 'Where's your goggles, ref?'

Teams inevitably suss out the easiest way of scoring a goal. With a scoop into the air, a player can head or volley the ball into the net, with the crowd cheering regardless of who scores. Another tactic favoured for scoring is to direct throwins straight at the goal. Further action close to the goal creates a scramble among the players as the attacking team relentlessly kicks the ball until the onslaught succeeds in pushing the ball over the line – if anyone can tell, that is, through the melee.

The teams swap ends at half-time, with towels and hairdryers passed around, enabling the prima donnas to maintain their good looks. The floodgates open in the second half as the game ebbs and flows, with a deluge of goals ever more likely.

Professional conduct wavers as tiredness spreads through the team and the novelty of the playing surface wears thin. Players resort to blatant barging and even shirt-tugging to repossess the ball, and even off the ball expect to see players pushed into the water. Play is also directed more at the crowd, with many spectators unwittingly brought into the action if they are looking too dry.

The final whistle brings relief to spectators and players alike, with the game normally ending in a draw (only because everyone has lost count). Even in August, after 30 minutes drenched to the skin, players stand physically frozen and swiftly squelch off the pitch to avoid an irate and drenched bystander. Meanwhile, the referee heads off to the football club to wet his whistle.

HISTORY

The match has taken place for around 70 years, and it's believed to have first started after some local lads were bored and decided to add some spice to their football match. The idea obviously caught on, with Whitsun the original date for the match. The game continued throughout the war, with the teams including members of the RAF, based nearby.

The event is now a fundraiser for the local team, and raises around £2,000. The modern game has seen a few subtle changes, including bringing the goals closer together and even a match sponsor, but the game has yet to make an appearance on *Splash of the Day*!

The referee hasn't always worn the traditional black kit, and back in the 1950s he turned up for one match wearing ladies' clothes and carrying an umbrella, which in those days was extremely brave, earning him extra splashes no doubt.

ESSENTIALS

There's only one game every year, exclusively for players of Bourton Football Club. While most games are six-a-side, teams can be bigger if there's sufficient interest from the club. Spectators should arrive well in advance of the kick-off for a vantage point on either bridge or along the sidelines: just take heed of anyone dressed head-to-toe in waterproofs. If you insist on bringing along a camera, be very quick to move; the more expensive the camera looks, the more likely the players will splash it!

TIPS

For spectators, be ready to run when the ball heads towards you. The crowd will get soaked as play edges nearer to the riverbank. For a chance to play in the game, you will have to move to Bourton-on-the-Water and become a regular in the town's football team.

WACKY FACT

A few years ago, one player turned up sporting armbands and snorkel, although a wetsuit would perhaps have been more appropriate.

IF YOU LIKE THIS

For another absurd football game, try swamp football. The Swamp Soccer New World Championships takes place in Strachur, Argyll, Scotland. The game was originally conceived by cross-country skiers in Finland in 1997, but the Scottish game is played by six-a-side teams in a wet bog/mud-sodden pitch. There are male, female and mixed team tournaments, but don't expect to see too much Beckhamesque skill!

SHEEP GRAND NATIONAL

'Don't get fleeced by the bookie!'

Location: The Big Sheep, near Bideford, North Devon

Date: A Saturday in early April (Grand National Day)

Time: 3.45pm

Entry fee: From £5

Further information:
www.thebigsheep.co.uk

Grid reference: SS 427 265

Spectator Fun: ★★★★

Wackiness: ★★★★

Family Friendly: ★★★★★

$$\text{————————}\left(\text{WHAT HAPPENS}\right)\text{————————}$$

Forget the Derby, Royal Ascot and Glorious Goodwood – the big event in the racing calendar takes place in Devon, where Little Pullover and Red Ram are two of the fastest-trotting sheep in Britain, competing in the prestigious Grand National Sheepstakes.

The crowds flock to the racecourse in best hats and frocks, clutching their form guide and eyeing up the latest odds, although there are very few clues offered from the sheep themselves, who saunter past at a snail's pace under the beady eye of Craig, the sheepdog.

The lightweight jockeys saddle up at the starting post, including the legendary Woolly Carson, Bob Chump and Jester Piglet. Bob Chump, riding Alderknitty, is a little the worse for wear after belatedly tumbling out of the jockeys' bar, and struggles to mount his frisky ewe, before finally grabbing hold of the reins. Meanwhile, Little Pullover's jockey had last pick of the racing silks, and looks very sheepish in a little pink number.

There's a last-minute flurry of £1 bets as Honest Joe, the local bookmaker, pulls the wool over punters' eyes, slyly recommending everyone to 'back Woolly Jumper', which has a reputation for being the donkey in the pack. Red Ram and Sheargar attract the smart money, and it's 14/1 baa the rest of the field.

Runners and riders are all itching for the off (or is that the lice?) and the tension turns up a few woolly notches with plenty of jostling at the start line. Red Ram threatens to false-start, but a couple of barks from Craig sorts her out, while Bob Chump regrets having had that third glass of champagne

and is in danger of falling off before the race has even started. Then, under starter's orders, or whenever Craig decides to back off, Woolly Carson shouts out 'Last one home is a roast dinner', and the runners pick up the whiff of sheep nuts and fly down the course ... or at least as far as the first clump of grass they arrive at!

The race is seven sheepy furlongs, about 250 yards, and spectators lining the narrow course cheer in 'shear' delight as Sheargar lives up to the reputation of her equine namesake, making an early bolt for the front. The runners negotiate Bo Peep's Bend and Shepherd's Brook while resisting the temptation of a quick munch in the hedgerow. Little Pullover decides she doesn't have the stomach to race, and the lure of some grass is far more appealing – that is, if she can avoid the gaze of the sheepdog who prowls behind. A jockey wearing pink was never going to win anyway!

©The Big Sheep

Woolly Jumper surprises Honest Joe and even herself, entering the back straight as the clear leader with the jockey furiously cracking the whip. Sheargar is nowhere in sight, with rumours spreading like manure of a possible sheep-nap! Red Ram, the joint favourite (especially with some mint sauce), is right on the tail of Woolly Jumper, making it a two-sheep race. Meanwhile Golden Fleece, with four left feet, is now going backwards – regrettably for the punters, who wish that they'd staked an each-way bet.

The sheep make the crucial final swing at Ewe's Turn, before entering the home straight with the challenge of clearing three tricky jumps, all at least twenty inches high. Woolly Jumper makes the first of the jumps tentatively, but once over the line of baby conifers, the prize of a bucket of food enters her radar and she skips nonchalantly over the next hurdle.

There are no fallers at the first jump, although Golden Fleece decides to stop for a chomp and proceeds to chew half the fence before carrying on.

Red Ram hesitates at the second fence, nearly sending Jester Piglet somersaulting (if it's good enough for Frankie Dettori ...) into the champagne-swigging Tattersall enclosure. The chasing pack gain ground and it looks like the race will be a dead heat, until a late surge from Woolly Jumper, no stranger to sheep dips, who lunges over the finishing line to win the race in a blistering fifteen seconds and leaves spectators speechless. Jester Piglet bleats a sigh of relief as he just about clings on to his mount to cross the line in second place, while Bob Chump is left trailing in the mud and sheep muck and reaches the end fit only for the washing machine. Meanwhile, back at the start, Little Pullover is still happily munching the grass, blissfully unaware that the race is all over.

The cuddly, fluffy jockeys have no opportunity to dismount as the sheep ignore all cameras and interviews and plough straight for the food. The crowd are jubilant after backing the long shot Woolly Jumper, and give chase as Honest Joe hastens his exit. Unfortunately there's no time for too much celebration, as sheep and jockeys are back in action tomorrow. A few days later, Sheargar's trainer receives a 'ramsom' note for the sheep's release!

HISTORY

The races have been going for over twenty years, but they don't always run to script. Sheep have plenty of off days when running, and jumping is simply not on the cards. Approaching the first of the jumps, the sheep have been known to pull up and run backwards, but usually a growl or two from the resident sheepdog sends them running the right way again. The sheepdog has even raced alongside to quicken the pace!

The Sheepstakes Grand National very nearly became a piggyback race one year when ewes and rams inadvertently found themselves in the same enclosure, probably the work of a disgruntled punter keen to upset the odds. Organisers have resisted the temptation to replicate the original Grand National course too much, fearing that the sheep, upon reaching the infamous Becher's Brook, would prefer to drink the water instead of hurdling over it.

The woollen sheep jockeys had a break one year, but Jester and Bob were outraged that fluffy dogs were their replacements, and successful protests saw them unanimously reinstated!

ESSENTIALS

Betting is a mug's game, but spectators are allowed to make £1 bets on any of the sheep, with the prize of a mug should their sheep win. Honest Joe doubles up as the race commentator, building up the tension and providing an hilarious commentary on the race until he's too hoarse to speak. Besides the Grand National, there's a race on the same course every day between March and October, and the sheep swap over halfway through the season for a deserved break from the racing.

The Big Sheep is a woolly theme park with plenty of attractions – just as long as you like all things ovine – but for those who prefer their lambs served up on a plate, there are also duck trials, a horse-whispering show and an outdoor laser shooting game (no shooting at the sheep).

TIPS

Watch out for Honest Joe, who will lead you up the garden path with some of his tips. Woolly Jumper has a reputation for being a slow runner and usually comes last, while on a hot sunny day when the going is 'as hard as concrete', always back Red Ram – but avoid betting on Alderknitty if you notice Bob Chump looking legless. Then again, form usually goes out of the window, so back all six sheep to be sure of taking home a mug!

WACKY FACT

Punters from as far as Wales and Yorkshire have phoned to place genuine bets on the race, but they feel a right mug when told what actually happens.

IF YOU LIKE THIS

Hoo Farm near Telford, Shropshire (www.hoofarm.com) hosts a Grand National in May for sheep and goats. There's also Derby Day in June, besides the regular Sheep Steeple-chase and Galloping Goats race, held daily. There's another annual sheep race on the Channel Island of Sark, every July.

The Mascot Grand National is yet another mad take on the horse race, contested at Huntingdon racecourse in Cambridgeshire every October. Cuddly mascots belonging to sports clubs, organisations and charities, including Pudsey Bear, Harry the Hornet and Wacky Macky Bear, compete over a series of hurdles on a one-furlong course. The event has run alongside the horseracing since 1999, and one year there was controversy when the winner, Freddie the Fox, was disqualified after being outed as an Olympic athlete!

Finally, every November, in aid of Children in Need, Birmingham hosts the Pantomime Horse Grand National.

REAL ALE WOBBLE

'Leave your Chopper or three-gear racer at home!'

Location:	Llanwrtyd Wells, Powys
Date:	A weekend in mid-November
Time:	Registration from 8.30am
Entry fee:	£22 for two days (£16 for either day)

Further information:
www.green-events.co.uk

Grid reference: SN 878 467

Spectator Fun:	★
Wackiness:	★
Pain Factor:	★★★
Training Required:	★★★★
Family Friendly:	★

WHAT HAPPENS

This is probably the muddiest 'pub crawl' in Britain, and arguably the most scenic; if you get a chance to admire it, that is. Organised by the same man who brought you the Bog Snorkelling contest, and with the course designed by mountain bikers, there will never be a dull moment!

Competitors tackle arduous hill climbs and mud-ridden paths on mountain bikes, stopping at various points along the way to taste a selection of local beers. There are three routes available for cyclists: fifteen miles for the beer drinkers, and 25 or 35 miles for those with a propensity for pain or getting dirty. All three routes meander through the Welsh countryside, inclusive of mud, hills and more mud. The variety of the terrain taken depends on how much ale you drink, and towards the end expect some off-piste cycling!

There's no set start time, with everyone gathering in the town square for a briefing and, more importantly, to pick up beer tokens before racing off. The majority of the entrants are serious mountain bikers, suitably attired in Lycra from head to foot, with a few bulging calf muscles in between. Others, who obviously misread the clothing requirements, arrive more appropriately dressed for the beer-drinking pit stops, with jeans and even a fairy costume worn by a couple of naive participants.

There's a very relaxed start, but expect the more competitive to race ahead, leaving behind the recreational entrants. The initial couple of miles allow cyclists to bed themselves in, offering false optimism that the day will pass by pain-free.

Competitors soon stretch out along the route, and while the Lycra-clad cyclists have reached the first drinks station, the stragglers are still ascending the first of many hills. Around every bend another interminable climb comes into view, and many routinely dismount, walk for a short stretch and then attempt to cycle further, before repeating the process, while wondering whether their bike has a reverse gear only. On the 'upside', camaraderie develops between the back-markers, who together find the energy to struggle to the top, although at the back of everyone's minds is the old adage, 'What goes up ...'

After a brief interlude on the flat, potholes become the bugbear, with novices perhaps wishing they had at least worn padded shorts and chosen a bike with more suspension. Having swerved around as many holes as possible, there's little time for the backside to recover before yet another potential disaster greets the cyclists: a near-precipitous drop through a wooded section (and still no sign of the first beer stop). There's a unanimous curse of Gordon Green, the race organiser, together with half-baked promises of exacting revenge later on.

Dismounting is the only sensible option for novices to negotiate this part of the course without vaulting over the handlebars. Even walking the bike is not as easy as it sounds, as other cyclists uncontrollably pass by, skidding with every turn, wishing they too had got off and walked, but now finding themselves beyond the point of braking and losing all volition. Seconds later, there's a dull thud, followed by a clang and a faint groan, that could possibly be the sound of a cyclist striking a tree!

The first beer stop brings much-welcomed relief for the majority, that's if they can stomach the dark ale that looks suspiciously similar to the local river. Fortunately, appearances belie the taste, and cyclists are quickly invigorated with a warm glow which lasts until the next catastrophe or tantrum. There are several beers available for sampling, and the stop offers a chance to recharge batteries, change into the first set of spare clothing after this regrettable moment of lunacy, and share stories of mishaps already experienced. There's even the option of seeing your friends head out on one of the two extra loops (including an extra beer stop), while you wait for their return and admire the rain. Though they may not be your friends on their return!

A few hours later and back on the road there are further obstacles, now made far trickier after the beer, including a small stream to fall into (many throw a wobbly here!) and a steep drop to plunge down. The latter tempts most cyclists to approach at full pelt … just avoid the front brakes! Luckily, along the whole course there are well-placed first aid stations on hand should anyone decide to try some acrobatics, but don't expect the first-aiders to repair flat tyres or straighten wheels. Those who are cold and weary could perhaps feign an injury and be chauffeured back to town in an ambulance.

Towards the end, the Wobble becomes a ramble as calf muscles ache and the last set of spare clothing is soaked through. Those who have had three beers and a few hairraising moments are glad to arrive back in town safely. Most participants manage to complete the circuit in around five hours, still with plenty of time for further beer stops in town. Unfortunately, for those crazy enough to cycle for a second day, there's more misery yet to come.

HISTORY

One of a huge number of activities introduced to Llanwrtyd Wells over the last 25-odd years by Gordon Green MBE. In the first year of the Wobble, a local reporter got wind of it and wrote an article about an event involving cyclists drinking lots of beer and then heading out onto the public highway. A few days later, Gordon received a stern phone call from the police, but luckily, after a brief explanation, the event still went ahead as planned. The Wobble takes place alongside the Mid-Wales Beer Festival, one of the longest beer festivals in Britain.

ESSENTIALS

The registration is where you will receive the beer tokens, with the briefing and start outside the Neuadd Arms in the main town square at approximately 10am. The ride is 'non-competitive', although there will always be a few enthusiastic cyclists speeding past.

There are two beer stops for those on the shortest route, and a third beer available for anyone brave enough to cycle on one of the two longer routes. Unfortunately, in the interests of wildlife safety, cyclists cannot drink more than three beers during the day, otherwise stories would circulate of tormented squirrels being chased through the woods by hordes of insane bikers. First aid and edible refreshments are available at each drinks stop, but expect lengthy queues at both and be prepared for a shortage of chips towards the end!

A good mountain bike is essential. Bring plenty of spare clothing, especially if you intend to take part on both days, and arrive prepared for all weathers, as it can be very cold and wet. Helmets are of course compulsory, while tool kits, gloves, knee and ankle pads, extra padding for your rear end and waterproofs are essential additions. Slower cyclists may also wish to pack a tent and sleeping bag. Hosepipes are available at the finish ... for the bikes and the muddier finishers!

Bikes can be hired from Cycles Irfon (01591 610668) and the local playing fields are open to campers for the weekend, with shower facilities in the sports club. There's plenty of live entertainment during the evening, including an impressive array of ales and ciders. Watch out for the 8.5% ale, which is sensibly not available out on the Wobble!

TIPS

The route changes from year to year, but to complete the Wobble in one piece some mountain biking experience is useful for safely negotiating the steep or slippery sections (usually at the same time). Fitness is also essential, but anyone with the bare minimum of experience should opt for the shorter distance of fifteen miles and walk the bike through any difficult sections ... unless you don't mind drinking your beer through a straw in a hospital bed. For those taking part on both days, add some headache tablets to your puncture repair kit!

WACKY FACT

There was panic one year when the weather was so cold that the beer along the course was almost frozen!

IF YOU LIKE THIS

The World Mountain Bike Bog Snorkelling Championships and the Mountain Bike Chariot Racing Championships, both held in Llanwrtyd Wells, are logical next stops after the Wobble. For a much slower pace of wild drinking, opt for the Real Ale Ramble instead. This also takes place during the festival, a week later – does anything normal ever happen in the town?

WORLD RUSSIAN EGG ROULETTE CHAMPIONSHIPS

'Prepare to be shell-shocked!'

Location: Thorpe Latimer Park, Swaton, near Sleaford, Lincolnshire. Between Helpringham and Swaton on the B1394

Date: A Sunday in late June (part of the Swaton Vintage Fair)

Time: From 1pm

Entry fee: Admission to fair (about £4 per adult) but free to enter the championship

Further information: www.eggthrowing.com

Grid reference: TF 132 397

Spectator Fun:	★★★★
Wackiness:	★★★★
World Champion:	★★★★★
Pain Factor:	★★
Training Required:	★
Family Friendly:	★★★

WHAT HAPPENS

Inspired by the 1970s film *The Deer Hunter*, with eggs replacing bullets in a surprisingly tense but very crackbrained contest. Anyone expecting a casino and some Eastern Europeans will be very disappointed.

The challenge is 'egg-stremely' simple: six eggs, five hard-boiled and one raw. Two contestants in turn choose an egg to smash on their forehead, with whoever opts for the raw one the very messy loser. The winner proceeds through to the next round of a knockout tournament, hoping Lady Luck doesn't desert them.

Competitors sit at opposite ends of a table, each sporting a bandana with an apt name such as Egghead, Egg-stream or Humpty. Before the contest begins, the combatants attempt to psych each other out with some aggressive grimaces and an exchange of wisecracks. Then, after the toss of a coin, tension mounts as the first of the competitors receives a tray of six near-identical eggs.

The eggs may not be touched or fondled prior to making a selection. Only a brief visual inspection is possible, but this doesn't preclude some futile deliberation. The game is 99 per cent luck, although scrutinising the egg for cracks, differences in colour or shape (due to boiling), and even the amount of fluff on the shell may offer some clues as to which eggs are hard-boiled. Of course any tactics must also take into consideration the possibility that officials have tampered with the eggs in an attempt to outwit devious competitors.

Eagle eyes scan the six eggs, each one closely perused before the competitor finally plucks up the courage to grasp one. With signs of worry on the face, a nervous hand carries the egg agonisingly towards the forehead. The sound of hard egg white and yolk crumbling away on impact brings palpable relief, with a victorious roar and a snarl across the table. The now despondent-looking opponent takes their turn, but rather than hesitating over the five remaining eggs, nonchalantly dives in without too much speculation and thrusts the egg towards the head. Another successful crush sees jeers and raised fists reciprocated across the table.

The theatrics continue as each player takes a turn, hearts pounding as the eggs are slowly whittled down. Eventually one of the competitors selects a much lighter-feeling egg, immediately overcome with a sense of foreboding. Sure enough, the 'yolk' is on them as the shell breaks in two on the forehead, followed by yellow slime abseiling down their face and body, and the winner jubilantly progresses through to the next round.

Sometimes the battle will come down to the last two eggs, and competitors have a 50-50 chance of success. Should the fifth egg prove to be hard-boiled, the unlucky player who has to select the final, uncooked egg must go through the motions even though they already know that they will end up with egg on their face.

HISTORY

Just eight participants took part in the inaugural contest in 2007, although there were many more volunteers eager to take part. James Bamber took the inaugural title, beating a granny from Peterborough, with the contest featuring on news and sport shows throughout the world, even making it onto CNN. The granny has vowed to return to get her revenge, and plans to spend less time baking and more time hard-boiling eggs in the meantime!

ESSENTIALS

The contest takes place alongside the Swaton Vintage Fair, where vintage cars, racing terriers and showjumping spaniels are on display. If that's still not enough 'egg-joyment', there's the Egg Relay, involving two teams of eleven who must pass twelve eggs along a distance of 100 metres, and the highlight of the fair, the World Egg Throwing Championships (see page 196).

TIPS

Winning the toss is crucial, and whoever goes first always has the odds stacked in their favour. Don't forget to rehearse those threatening looks beforehand, as the contest is also about putting off your opponent.

WACKY FACT

Andy Dunlop, egg-head honcho, is so determined to see eggs become extinct in Lincolnshire that he is adding yet another event called the Egg Trebuchet, involving a home-made machine to hurl the eggs. Maybe there should be an egg-laying contest to replenish stocks? Andy even had the audacity to invite US actor George Clooney to the 2008 competition after hearing that George built his own trebuchet to fire eggs at the paparazzi. Sadly, George failed to reply to the lucrative offer!

IF YOU LIKE THIS

Peterlee, near Durham, hosts the World Jarping Championship on Easter Monday, where hard-boiled eggs are used in a variation on the game of conkers, but without the string. In a knockout format, each competitor holds an egg in their hand and the aim is to crack your opponent's egg, requiring nothing more than a powerful and accurate flick of the wrist. Losers have the consolation of eating a slightly messy hard-boiled egg for supper, although those competitors who coated their egg in nail varnish to improve their chances of winning may be more reluctant to do so.

WORLD CUSTARD PIE THROWING CHAMPIONSHIPS

'That's another fine mess you've got me into!'

Location:	Detling Showground, Maidstone, Kent
Date:	A Saturday in June
Time:	From 1pm
Entry fee:	£40 per team
Further information:	www.wcpc.me.uk
Grid reference:	TQ 801 590

Spectator Fun:	★★★
Wackiness:	★★★
World Champion:	★★★
Pain Factor:	★
Training Required:	★
Family Friendly:	★★★★

WHAT HAPPENS

The action comes thick and fast in a very messy contest, where fans of slapstick comedy will be favourites to beat the cowardly custards!

It's pie heaven as teams of four clown around in an almighty custard pie fight. The aim is to score points, based on where the pie strikes the opposition, with top marks for a direct hit on the face. Unfortunately, teams may not bring along their own splurge gun!

Each team member begins with five pies in the heats, thrown with their weaker hand, definitely passing the advantage to ambidextrous competitors. Further stipulations require the pie to be flat on the palm and, prior to launch, below shoulder level. Teams must also stand at least eight feet three inches apart when they throw, although judges will be busy enough trying to keep track of the scores while avoiding wayward shots.

Disappointingly, the custard pies don't contain custard, which ricochets on impact and is therefore unsuitable for the contest. Instead, each of the 3,000-odd custard pies consists of flour, food colouring, water, and a clandestine ingredient which adds the 'pow' factor into the contest but remains a closely-guarded secret. Teams should avoid making any complaints about lumps in the custard, unless they fancy receiving a premature splat courtesy of the chef.

After the formalities of a parade of the teams (and maybe a quick taste of the pies), the first two teams loiter mischievously near tables filled with custard pies, discussing last-minute tactics. The onslaught commences, with the first pie finding its target with a resounding splat and a sharp shriek

from the recipient, never again to moan about slow service! In response, a pie heads in the opposite direction, with the thrower shouting 'Take splat!' for added effect. Thereafter, teams eschew all table manners for complete custard chaos and a free-for-all to make as much mess as possible.

The battle ensues, but any plans the teams devise are soon jettisoned and it's simply a case of grab and smash, as unbridled, puerile excitement takes over. The odd competitor attempts the rapid-fire method, aiming to pummel the target with all five pies at once, believing the opposition would never suspect such a daring ploy. Unfortunately, if the first pie misses, the next four are likely to follow suit.

The rules allow for only three feet of manoeuvrability, and as the custard pies fly in from all directions and angles, recipients of the pies can duck, cower, turn their back, or scream like a big girl. But they soon realise that attack is the best form of defence, and give as good as they get. They do, though, have the luxury of blocking shots with their arm, but only from above the elbow.

Competitors also struggle to cleanly dispatch the custard pie, as the thin crust prematurely disintegrates in their hand; and once fired into the air, the missile only manages to shower the opposition with fragments of custard.

The eight-foot gap between the teams gradually narrows as both sets of players advance menacingly, arms impossibly extended, until the custard pie is within licking distance of the target. Competitors inevitably overstep the mark as they foray further into enemy territory and find themselves disqualified.

The allocation of five pies per player soon runs out, and scraps of pastry and handfuls of gloop are all that remain. These are frantically scooped up and sprayed at the opposition in

the futile hope of securing some last-minute points. Officials put everyone out of their misery and end the bombardment before teams resort to throwing the tables.

The judges total up the scores somehow, but a look at the amount of custard on both teams' clothing is a sure-fire way to determine the winners. As the first of the teams exit the arena, the next competitors eagerly await further custard warfare, but now with the added hazard of a slippery floor. The later rounds of the championship involve even more pies for the competitors to hurl at one another.

HISTORY

The original contest took place in 1967 in Coxheath to raise funds for the village hall, and after a protracted interlude since 1987, it returned to Maidstone in 2007 for its 40th anniversary. The Charlie Chaplin film *Behind the Screen* was the original inspiration for the contest – luckily, the founder wasn't a fan of *Zulu*! In the early years, only male teams could enter, but women were included … as the targets. After many complaints, women finally got the chance to compete.

Buster Keaton, who was one of the original innovators of custard pie throwing, bestowed on himself the title of first World Champion. He even had his own baking tactics, including cooking a double crust to ensure the pie didn't crumble before take-off, although there are no double crusts, or even tin foil containers, in the World Championships!

ESSENTIALS

Teams receive or lose points depending on the accuracy of the throwing. A direct hit on the face receives six points, near misses above the shoulder get three points, and one point is awarded for a body hit. Should anyone completely miss twice in a row, the team will lose one point, and judges even award extra points for the most imaginative throwing technique without breaking any rules. The rules fail to mention how many points are scored for a splatter on the face of one of the judges. Competitors can handle only three pies at any one time, although anyone who can successfully launch more than three at once deserves extra points for dexterity.

Prior to the main action, the teams have some early opportunities to collect bonus points for the best fancy dress, based on a theme set by the organisers (2008 was 1940s costume), which poses a conundrum for competitors. Do they dress to impress the judges, or arrive in clothing designed to withstand the rigours of the contest – perhaps a giant serviette or bib?

A maximum of 24 teams can compete (the original contest attracted over 80 teams), but given its popularity, enter early to guarantee a place. The organisers accept no responsibility should any innocent bystanders receive custard in the face. On the same afternoon (but not at the same time, unfortunately), there is a Welly Throwing Contest, a Skipping Competition, and even the UK Egg Throwing Championships – that is, if there are any eggs left after the chef has made all the custard pies.

TIPS

Obviously, power and pinpoint accuracy are essential, but for extra points, teams will need to be more cunning. Diagonal chucks are the best way to catch the opposition unawares – or wait until your target has released their pie before firing back and catching them at their most susceptible for a facial splatter.

Buster Keaton had many techniques for throwing a custard pie. The 'Ancient Roman discus throw' requires the thrower to spin around before letting go of the pie, and the 'Catcher's throw to second base' involves pulling the arm back before the release.

Finally, sit through hours of slapstick comedies to study the masters in action. The Laurel and Hardy film *Battle of the Century* sees a staggering 3,000 custard pies thrown!

WACKY FACT

In 1998, 50 members of the Laurel and Hardy Fan Club participated in the largest-ever custard pie fight, when 4,400 pies were thrown in three minutes. Meanwhile, in 2006, American Kelly Rida threw 24 custard pies at a human target in one minute, which still stands as a world record. Let's hope Kelly never enters a team in the World Championships!

IF YOU LIKE THIS

The World Black Pudding Throwing Championships in Ramsbottom, Lancashire offers another opportunity to launch food at a target, but without the mess or the threat of the food coming back at you (see page 289).

WAITERS' AND WAITRESSES' RACES

'Waiter, there's no beer in my glass!'

Location: Dartmouth, South Devon

Date: A Friday in late August

Time: From 9am

Entry fee: None

Further information:
www.dartmouthregatta.co.uk

Grid reference: SX 878 513

Spectator Fun: ★★★

Wackiness: ★★

Pain Factor: ★

Training Required: ★

Family Friendly: ★★★★

WHAT HAPPENS

Waiters and waitresses require ample athleticism and coordination as they compete for the ultimate bartending accolade. Fortunately, the entrants won't have to contend with drunken louts, bum-pinching lechers or randomly plonked tables and chairs, but there are the judges to keep happy.

Competitors run up and down a short course in Dartmouth, and in between they face the potentially embarrassing task of pouring a can of beer. The waiters and waitresses compete in separate races, but that doesn't preclude a couple of male entrants in drag attempting to enter alongside the barmaids; however, even if the hairy legs and bristles evade the officials, a flawlessly opened can of beer will soon oust them as imposters.

The waitresses are off first, many tactically dressed in judge-pleasing short skirts as they sprint to the end of the road clutching an empty pint glass and tray in each hand. Speed is the key on the first half of the course and dexterity crucial for the run back to the finish, but the halfway stage demands consummate bartending qualities, requiring competitors to spend as little time as possible filling their glass with as much beer as they can.

Unbeknown to the competitors, crafty officials hovering around the table at the halfway mark add some extra froth to the proceedings by shaking up the cans beforehand, catching out some of the waitresses, who lurch back with a shriek as a fountain of beer sprays out.

The cocktail-bar waitresses exhibit imprudence as they tip the entire contents of the can into the glass, only to regret their temerity as the froth rises up and over, accompanied by

tut-tutting from the men watching the race, lamenting the wastage. Other entrants show too much caution, trickling the beer into the glass. The rules prevent competitors from taking the can of beer on the run back to the finish, and as the head of froth refuses to settle in the glass, impatience gets the better of the waitresses, who are forced to rejoin the race, reluctantly leaving behind the half-empty cans of bitter.

The return leg requires entrants to hold the tray and glass of beer with the necessary deportment and poise. Supporting the glass with the flat palm of the hand, waitresses gingerly trot back with their free hand outstretched for balance, casting worried glances at the beer that sloshes precariously close to the rim.

Those crossing the finishing line first return with a pitiful amount of beer, but regardless of how quickly the course is completed, it's the competitor finishing with the most beer in the glass who is declared the winner (as long as they come in the first six). The glasses of beer are served to the judges, who complain about the poor service before bringing out a ruler to measure how much beer remains, although it's probably quicker to just count the number of dribbles!

Genuine waiters are thin on the ground in the men's race, with chefs, Navy recruits and blonde-bewigged imposters lining up on the start line, with not a waistcoat or bow-tie in sight. The sprint to the cans of beer causes early trouble for the drag acts, who struggle to carry the trays and glasses while hoicking up their dresses and keeping their bosoms under control. Reaching the halfway point, the men effortlessly attack the cans, betraying many a night spent on the couch with a four-pack. Applying the exact angle of tilt and optimum speed for pouring, they faultlessly fill the glasses with barely a drop of beer spilt, although there are a few complaints that the beers aren't chilled!

More devious waiters decide to keep hold of the can as they run back, brazenly sneaking in extra beer along the way, but under the glare of suspicious officials, foul play is easily spotted. Most of the competitors forget waiter etiquette, adopting ungainly postures as they struggle to cope with multi-tasking. There's even a spot of boisterousness as rival competitors representing the Navy resort to some unsports-manlike shirt-tugging, behaviour expected more from drunken customers than the waiters! The competitors in drag continue to the bitter end despite the sartorial hindrance, and even with their blonde wigs and spectacularly voluptuous figures, tips aren't very forthcoming from the judges!

Measurements from the first six in the waiter race are a lot closer (it's amazing there's any beer left at all!) and the judges are keen to introduce a beer-tasting tie-breaker should there be any dead heats. Coming home last, one local waiter delivers a perfectly full glass of beer with his dignity intact but is destined for a job behind the bar, leaving the running and fetching to the quicker waitresses!

HISTORY

The Waiters' and Waitresses' Race first took place in 1985 as an addition to the Dartmouth Royal Regatta, a week-long fes-tival of events, competitions and displays that began in 1822. In 1856 Queen Victoria made an unscheduled stop in Dartmouth on the eve of the Regatta due to bad weather, and before leaving bestowed the title of 'Royal'. Every year the town requests royal patronage, and the current patron is the Duke of York.

Apart from representatives of the Royal Navy, foreign warships often dock at Dartmouth during the Regatta and compete in the madcap races. One in particular is the Belgian fleet, who arrive in the smallest of the warships but always perform admirably in the races.

ESSENTIALS

The races take place from the Boatfloat Bridge to Birssy's Bar on the estuary front – just head for the sound of smashing glasses! Only employees working in the bars and restaurants in Dartmouth and the surrounding towns are usually eligible to take part (but the organisers may use their discretion), which means that you will need to get a job in the area first. Winners receive a small cash prize and a bottle of champagne. There's another prize for the best costume, while every bar in Dartmouth will inundate the winners with job offers afterwards. The losers find themselves banished to the kitchen!

On the same morning (dubbed 'Fun and Games' morning), there's a Barrel Rolling Race and the International Shopping Trolley Grand Prix. The Barrel Rolling involves teams of four who must use only their hands to move the barrel; just stand well back from the road if you watch – the barrels can and will go anywhere (especially if the inebriated waiters are involved). The Trolley Grand Prix is open to children and adults, with each team comprising a mechanic and a driver, but instead of filling the trolley with food, teams must refuel with water to ensure they make it to the finishing line. If all that sounds like too much action, there's also a Crab Catching Contest and a pavement artists' competition.

TIPS

Unfortunately, there will be no tips for competitors during the races. The main tactic is not to get too much 'a head'! Time your final sprint to the finish to arrive in fifth or sixth place, allowing a slower run but with more time for filling the glass and avoiding spillages. This is a risky ploy, but for those with fast feet it's a chance worth taking.

The best tip for pouring the beer, according to experienced bartenders, is to 'slosh a small amount of beer in the glass first, then pour again, hopefully compacting the head and breaking any bubbles in the process. Tilt the glass to 45 degrees before gently aiming for the side of the glass, and empty the remainder of the can. As the beer rises up the glass, straighten the glass until the froth tips over the top.' In other words, less head and more speed!

As for the difficult part of carrying the beer, competitors may wish to compare their predicament to the feat of an Australian man who broke the world record in 2007 for serving twenty one-litre tankards of beer in one go, over a distance of 40 metres!

WACKY FACT

For many years, local twins have competed in the race disguised as elderly ladies, often raiding the local charity shop for floral dresses and false perms. How will they cope in the future when they have to race with Zimmer frames?

IF YOU LIKE THIS

There are other Waiters' and Waitresses' races in Salcombe, Devon and Ludlow, Shropshire. The latter has the distinction of sending the winner to compete in the International Waiters' Race in Ghent, Belgium, which challenges entrants to compete in the much more arduous, and potentially expensive, task of carrying a bottle of Pineau des Charentes liquor and three full glasses.

Edgworth Cricket Club near Bolton hosts the Lancashire Waiters' Dash Championship. The race is part of the local festival of food and culture, held in September. The World Gravy Wrestling Championships also take place during the week of the festival!

WORLD WINTER SWIMMING CHAMPIONSHIPS

'Its f-f-freezing in here!'

Location:	Various venues (usually somewhere very cold)
Date:	The coldest weekend of the year, held biennially
Time:	All weekend
Entry fee:	£25
Further information:	www.SLSC.org.uk and www.wwsc2008.com
Grid reference:	TQ 294 720 (in 2008)

Spectator Fun:	★★
Wackiness:	★★
World Champion:	★★
Pain Factor:	★★★★
Training Required:	★★★★
Family Friendly:	★★

WHAT HAPPENS

Hundreds of competitors take part in a series of breathtaking swimming races where the water temperature hovers barely above freezing. The contest may even improve your sex drive – that is, if you ever thaw out!

The main event is the 'Head-up Breaststroke' World Championships, requiring competitors to swim across one width of an unheated pool (approximately 25 metres) in the middle of winter. Many of those swimming are barrel-chested, vodka-drinking Russians and Finns who habitually put their bodies through the daily rigours of icy-cold water. For the rest, it's a matter of swimming fast enough to leave the pool before the body freezes. Unfortunately, the rules on swimming attire are strictly regimented and only trunks or a swimsuit are permitted, although there's nothing to say that men can't turn up in a polka-dot bikini!

In a series of heats, split into age groups, officials call six fully-clothed competitors to the poolside, many already palpitating with fear. The torment begins early when the swimmers are herded around the water's edge, discarding various articles of clothing as they go. The sight of polystyrene icebergs in the water does nothing to assuage the competitors' dread, and upon reaching the start line (if they don't run away first) there's an impressive set of goosebumps on display – and that's before they're even in the pool.

The compère has delight in poking fun at every competitor, with the greatest derision saved for anyone sporting a particularly laughable, or alluring, swimming costume. Just don't turn up in a pair of tight orange trunks – they won't be so tight at the finish! There's further concern from the novice cold-water swimmers when they hear the swimming credentials of their rivals, many of whom train in Siberia or have swum the English Channel.

Finally, competitors apprehensively dip their toes into the water before reluctantly jumping into their designated lane of the pool with a few shrieks and grimaces. Even the teeth begin to chatter in anticipation. After wading through the water with arms and upper body held aloft, officials request competitors to plunge their shoulders under the water, and as they do so, the shock whips away their breath, many perhaps wishing they were enjoying a hot bath with rubber ducks for company.

A count to three precedes the sound of the klaxon, although many have trouble hearing the start through their earplugs and headgear, leading to some comical send-offs. The rules require swimmers to keep their eyes above the water, with officials at the far end of the pool prepared to add on penalties should they see anyone try to gain an advantage. Other than that, as long as competitors attempt a recognisable form of breaststroke, anything else goes.

False starts are rare, but when they happen, the competitors continue to swim, oblivious of the waving arms, muttering to themselves: 'Damned if I'm going to go through this all over again!'

As the initial stinging subsides, the adrenalin rush abates any cowardly tendency to backtrack out of the pool. The swimming is fast and furious, arms and legs vigorously moving through the water lest they become frozen. Nearly everyone wears the same shocked expression, eyes and mouth agape in sheer bewilderment, transfixed by the finishing line. Despite the short length of the race, a gap quickly opens up and the competitors wearing cumbersome headgear soon find themselves adrift of the leader. Swimmers may also suffer the ignominy of seeing a competitor with a duck on their head breeze past in the outside lane.

Colourful and loud flag-waving supporters cheer on the Finnish, Russian and Slovak competitors. Sadly, the British supporters can barely look, shuddering at the thought of taking part. The race takes twenty-odd seconds but feels a lot longer for the competitors, who are in danger of turning the race into a dead heat, eventually touching the far end before bounding out of the pool, desperately flinging their hands out for a towel. They then face a life or death-by-hypothermia decision – do they jump into the hot tub or slip into the sauna?

The hardy Scandinavians boldly stride around in trunks all day, while the sound of chattering teeth and shivering limbs betrays the weak constitution of the British competitors, despite the ten layers of clothing. A few hours later, once the tingle effect has kicked in and warmth has returned to the hands, competitors head to the bar for a pint of Blue Tits or Chilly Willy, or in the case of the mad Finns, jump into the pool for another swim.

HISTORY

The World Championships came to Tooting Bec Lido in London for the first time in 2008, but they usually take place in much chillier climes (2006 was held in Finland), on behalf of the International Winter Swimming Association. Tooting Bec Lido, built in 1906, is the largest freshwater swimming pool in Europe, and is 100 yards long. However, there were a few grumblings of dissatisfaction among the Russians in 2008, who complained that 'the water in the pool was too warm and the hot tub water too cold'! The British competitors had the opposite complaint.

The lido has already hosted the British Cold Water Championships in 2006 and 2007, and there are faint murmurings of another British Championship in 2009 at the same venue – no excuses for those who find it too extravagant to travel across Europe to freeze in a pair of trunks.

ESSENTIALS

There are separate races for different age groups, precluding any chance of a 70-year-old having to compete against a Russian champion. Fastest times, and not position, in each age group decide which competitors make it to the final; so even if you win your heat, if the time was slow you may not make the final. Conversely, you could finish last in a race and still qualify for the final.

Alongside the main races, there's a freestyle race, relay race and synchronised swimming. There's even an endurance race, usually won by Lewis Gordon Pugh, who has completed long-distance swims at the North Pole and in the Antarctic as preparation. For those who would rather test their body's endurance without the complication of racing, there's a separate area of the pool available ... just watch out for those icebergs!

Wetsuits or clothing below the knee or shoulders are absolutely forbidden, as is anything else that may enhance performance and cut short the torture, such as flippers, a jet ski or even a dab of petroleum jelly (although officials are unlikely to check the nether regions for signs of a furtive layering of duck fat!). In other words, all competitors will suffer! Fortunately, officials make a concession to wearing hats, and besides the practical latex swim caps there are many outrageous hats on display, including stetsons, bowler hats and bobble hats.

TIPS

South London Swimming Club (based at Tooting Bec Lido) has a small number of year-round members, and joining the club would be the ideal way to prepare for the next World Championships. Regular swimming in rivers, lakes and seas will also build up resistance; but given the short distance, it's less about adjusting to the cold and more about arm and leg power – and, of course, an insane urge to enter.

It's advisable to keep away from the drinks bar unless you're definitely sure you won't make the final. In the words of one surprised competitor in 2007: 'I've had two pints and just realised I'm in the final in two hours' time!'

WACKY FACT

For those who need more persuasion to enter, cold-water swimming apparently boosts one's libido. There are also numerous supposed health benefits, including cures for depression and drooping breasts – though there has yet to be evidence of the latter among the men!

IF YOU LIKE THIS

The biennial World Championships moves around Europe, and will next take place in 2010 in the more scenic surroundings of Lake Bled in Slovenia (www.si-sport.com). Don't expect it to be unseasonably warm, as past contests have taken place in temperatures as low as minus 20°C, with officials breaking ice to create the swimming lanes. One of the funniest moments from previous World Championships was a team of Russian men performing *Swan Lake*, complete with the full ballerina garb – which even they found tutu cold!

WORLD BLACK PUDDING THROWING CHAMPIONSHIPS

'Swaddle yer puddings'

Location:	Royal Oak pub, Bridge Street, Ramsbottom, Lancashire
Date:	The second Sunday in September
Time:	From midday until late afternoon
Entry fee:	£1 per three lobs (unlimited entries)
Further information:	Royal Oak, 01706 822786
Grid reference:	SD 791 169

Spectator Fun:	★★
Wackiness:	★★
World Champion:	★★★★★
Pain Factor:	★
Training Required:	★
Family Friendly:	★★★★

WHAT HAPPENS

Inspired by the Wars of the Roses over 400 years ago, black puddings are hurled at a target of Yorkshire puddings – while later in the day, those who ate the black puddings end up hurling themselves!

For those unaccustomed to the northern *bonne bouche*, black pudding is dried pig's blood and suet wrapped in a stomach lining (surely it can't taste as offal as it sounds). The target is a stack of twelve giant Yorkshire puddings, balanced precariously on either side of a 30-foot-high plinth. Each competitor has three attempts to knock down as many Yorkshire puddings as possible, while obeying one rule: competitors may only throw underarm, handing the advantage over to the women.

Throws begin to the shout of 'Lob on!' and the first competitor eyes up the Yorkshire puddings (perhaps dreaming of a roast dinner) while keeping one foot in firm contact with the oche, placed 30 feet from the target. The standard approach is simply chucking the black pudding on top of the Yorkshire puddings, hoping that the impact will dislodge those that are overhanging. Others go for the basketball technique, throwing the pudding towards the back of the target, intending for the rebound to nick a pudding or two.

There are also plenty of duff attempts on display, with competitors failing to throw the black pudding high enough and perhaps wishing they could enter the junior category instead, where they only have to aim at a twenty-foot-high target. The throwing rules fail to deter the sneakier entrants from stooping to some furtive overarm lobs for extra power, but by the third chuck the officials have spotted the rule violation and disqualified them.

The best shots come from female and older entrants who choose accuracy over brute pudding force, managing to knock off at least one Yorkshire pudding. For the men who over-egg the black pudding, the projectile soars embarrassingly past the target, causing some concern for passers-by who find themselves in the unique situation of dodging flying black puddings (and hoping a leg of lamb isn't on its way).

Scores of one or two are regularly attained, but the much-sought-after 'pud-trick' is a rarity, and anyone who achieves a score in each of his or her three throws will probably finish at the top of the leaderboard.

With the highest score of the day a very beatable four Yorkshire puddings, the tension turns up a few notches. Competitors knocking off puddings with their first two shots

suddenly find themselves with an opportunity to take the overall lead. But the pressure of the third lob gets too much, and the Yorkshire puddings stubbornly remain balanced on the edge of the plinth while the competitor throws down his flat cap in frustration. Other contenders, who also get agonisingly close to a high score, bemoan the poor-quality black puddings, blaming their below-par chucks on insufficient suet and too much swaddling!

With every unsuccessful attempt the Yorkshire puddings inch ever closer to the edge, and eagle-eyed competitors who have bided their time now jump in to seek the most opportune moment to strike. Unfortunately, officials are quick to thwart any professional tactics and reposition the puddings on the centre of the plinth – much to the dismay of the competitor, who now has little chance of success.

Should there be a tie at the end of the day, competitors compete in a sudden-death lob-off until there's an outright

winner. In 2006, the event had a particularly tight finish when three men were level. After a game of paper, rock and scissors to determine the order of play, they all managed to score three in their initial shot. Even after the second lob there were still two people level, and it took three rounds for the winner to be decided. The men were very grateful that this wasn't an eating contest!

HISTORY

Whether true or not, there's the quixotic explanation that the idea came from a battle during the Wars of the Roses between the Houses of Lancaster and York. It's believed that Yorkshire ran out of ammunition and decided to prolong the battle with Yorkshire puddings. Lancashire, in retaliation, threw black puddings back, with perhaps the main casualties coming from over-indulgence rather than concussion. A less exciting explanation is that mill hands many years ago relieved the boredom during their lunch breaks by throwing leftover food at a makeshift target.

The competition began in the 1980s at the Corner Pin pub in nearby Stubbins, but on its closure moved to its present location in Ramsbottom. Before separate targets were set up for juniors, a seven-year-old jointly won the main contest in 2001. His exploits even inspired a character in an American comic.

Over 300 black puddings and 200 Yorkshire puddings are specially produced for the event, with extra puddings in cold storage should they run out. A few years ago, during a particularly wet afternoon, the Yorkshire puddings required regular changing as they metamorphosed into a pile of mush. The following year, organisers unwisely opted for frozen puddings, but competitors found them even harder to dislodge, resulting in some very low scores.

The competition has even attracted interest from gardeners, who entered a floral design, based around the Black Pudding Throwing, into a flower show. And in 2002 the contest became an unofficial event in the Commonwealth Games, held in nearby Manchester.

ESSENTIALS

Leading up to the event, a swaddling ceremony takes place, which involves wrapping the black puddings in ladies' hosiery. The tights add some durability to the projectiles, averting a splattering of the road – and the crowd – with pig fat.

The oche arrives at the venue with a military escort and to the tune of Scottish bagpipes. Also known as the Golden Grid, its history is unclear, although the initials LCC on the side indicate Roman origin. Then again, it could always stand for 'Lancashire County Council'.

There are twenty rules for the contest, including rule 13(a) which requires all competitors from Wigan to inform the officials beforehand, so that extra security can be arranged for the nearby pie shops; while rule 14 hints that bribing the officials with beer may give entrants a competitive edge.

Hot black puddings are on sale, and you can even choose between a fat or lean version, or just wait until the end and have as many cold, squashed puddings as you fancy. Competitors can throw vegetarian substitutes if they have ethical or religious opposition to using meat, or if anyone feels black puddings are too tasty to throw. Surprisingly, no one born outside Bury has any qualms about chucking them!

TIPS

There is another, more underhanded, tactic which a few knowledgeable entrants try. The platform which supports the Yorkshire puddings is loosely tied down and susceptible to a powerful shot from underneath. Such a shot could tilt the platform sufficiently to knock all twelve puddings off, breaking the world record and leaving the crowd in awe.

A further tip is to time your three throws to when the Yorkshire puddings are perilously close to dropping down, but don't leave it too late to jump in. Remember the key to success is accuracy and not power, so practise beforehand with whatever food you dislike the most, maybe throwing broccoli at a target of twelve tins of Spam.

WACKY FACT

The organisers are lobbying, tongue-in-cheek, to have the World Championships included in the 2012 London Olympics. They have even called their bid 'PudLondon' and re-designed the Team GB logo, replacing the Olympic rings with five Yorkshire puddings. They are garnering support across the wacky sports circuit, and one day Synchronised Pudding Throwing and the Lob, Skip and Jump will be top-drawer events.

IF YOU LIKE THIS

If your aversion to haggis (sheep's heart, lung and liver stuffed in a paunch) is even stronger than for black puddings, then Haggis Hurling is for you. Arbroath in Scotland hosts the archetypal Scottish contest during their Tartan Week celebrations in April. The current world record for throwing a haggis is over 180 feet, and has stood for over twenty years.

WORLD MARBLES CHAMPIONSHIP

'Whatever you do, don't lose your marbles'

Location: Greyhound Inn, Tinsley Green, West Sussex

Date: Good Friday (Marbles Day)

Time: From 10am until late

Entry fee: £24 per team

Further information: www.marblemuseum.org; Greyhound Inn, 01293 884220

Grid reference: TQ 288 395

Spectator Fun: ★★

Wackiness: ★★

World Champion: ★★★

Pain Factor: ★

Training Required: ★★★★

Family Friendly: ★★★

WHAT HAPPENS

The game of marbles may be a classic children's pastime, but the World Championships is anything but child's play. Watch out for some fudging and cabbaging, and just hope you don't get drawn against the Germans!

At the Wembley of the marble world, in yet another pub car park, teams of six gather around a concrete ring, six feet in diameter, with a gazebo on standby in the advent of a sudden downpour. In the centre of the sand-covered ring, there's a pack of 49 red target marbles, about half an inch in size. The aim of the game, known as Ringer, is to shoot your own marble (the tolley) at the pack and knock as many marbles out of the ring as possible, scoring a point for each one. First team to score 25 points wins.

A bizarre toss-up called the 'nose drop' precedes each game, which a newcomer to the competition could easily mistake for a nose-picking contest! The team captains stand over a line marked in the sand, and from their noses drop the tolley. The player with the marble nearest to the line has the choice to play first or second.

Players from each team take alternate turns at the ring. After a quick sweep and sanding of the arena by the referee, the first player limbers up, flexing his thumb and fingers before knuckling down, resting a minimum of one knuckle on the outside of the ring. Then, the hand contorts into the set position for flicking – the basic technique is to tuck the thumb under the middle finger and cradle the tolley on the index finger (palm up) – before letting the thumb loose, unleashing a venomous shot ... hopefully.

Style varies greatly, and more experienced players display intricate, often eccentric techniques, even lifting up one leg while they flick or cockily holding a beer in the other hand – these are usually the Australian competitors! First-timers, meanwhile, struggle to get to grips with the basics, realising that the game isn't as easy as they remembered!

The rules are quite simple. A player continues their turn if the tolley remains inside the ring and knocks at least one target marble out. If the tolley drops off the ring, even scoring points in the process, or remains on the ring without scoring, the play passes to the next player. The latter is often a tactical ploy, enabling the player to be closer to the action on their next turn and offering several scoring opportunities, as long as nobody stoops to gamesmanship and knocks their tolley back off!

The next player creaks down to the ringside to knuckle down, with the added comfort of a beer towel to cushion his arthritic knees. Shouts from the referee of 'On the edge!' forces the crafty competitor to drag the knuckle back to the correct spot on the edge of the ring. Squinting even harder to peruse all 49 marbles, he releases a pinpoint shot that mocks his doddering demeanour, scoring the first points in the match.

With the added bonus of holding the tolley inside the ring, experienced players can soon rack up a large break (the number of marbles knocked off in one turn) and even add spin to ensure that the tolley stays on the pitch. The player tiptoes over the marbles, squeezing his hand into the tightest of spaces for the next shot, and after scoring a few more points he eventually falls foul of bad luck. The player lambasts the referee for the quality of the pitch, before trundling back to his team, out of breath and threatening to give up marbles for the less energetic sports of tiddlywinks and dominoes.

Marbles wasn't a pastime we associated with blood sports – until, that is, a complete beginner approached the arena carrying a nasty-looking injury to his playing hand – a consequence of an over-enthusiastic training session on the treacherous practice ring, scraping the skin off his knuckles in the process. Leaving the pitch with trails of blood, he admitted: 'I never imagined a first aid kit would be needed for a game of marbles!'

With the marbles spread across the ring, there's much snooker-like deliberation, players painstakingly studying the myriad shots available. A group of marbles near the edge looks most appealing, and a player crouches down before nonchalantly knocking off three at once, earning tension-

relieving high fives from his team, the opposition looking on in disapproval of such loutish behaviour.

The rest of the game is tightly balanced, and nerves start to jangle more than the marbles as the score approaches the all-important 25 points. After the match, the victors protect their playing hands from all possible injury, cautiously offering handshakes to the losers and using their weaker hand for any menial chores, which could prove tricky in the toilets! The contest continues until late into the evening, by which time thumbs and marbles are well and truly battered and bruised.

HISTORY

The event officially started at the Greyhound pub in 1932, but contests took place many years previously. Sam Spooner was champion in the 1880s, and was still going strong in the

1930s, although his marbles were a bit the worse for wear by then. The local players dominated the early championships, but in recent years an intense rivalry has developed between England and Germany, pitting generations of marbling expertise against strict disciplinarians who train every day and probably even practise marble penalties just in case the final ends in a draw!

The tradition of playing marbles in Tinsley Green apparently goes back to Elizabethan times, when two rival men, from Surrey and Sussex, competed for the hand of a maiden. With no decisive result from contests in falconry, archery or wrestling, the two men turned to marbles to settle the matter. In 1922, a boy from New Jersey, USA was declared the first-ever marbles champion, until it was pointed out that a place called Tinsley Green in England had beaten them to the prestigious title by a few centuries. The Greyhound received a blue plaque in 2008, recognising it as a place of interest and safeguarding its future as a landmark in Sussex's sporting heritage.

Never complain about the state of the pitch, especially when competing against a team who are off their tolley! During a tense match many years ago, a highly volatile father and son were playing for one side when a player on the opposing team persistently muttered something along the lines of 'I think the pitch is too dry.' The father retorted, 'You want it wet?' and immediately threw his pint of beer all over the arena, followed by a deadly silence.

In the days when players counted their own marbles up, local legend Jim Longhurst, known as the Atomic Thumb, allegedly stuck clay to the soles of his shoes. When taking his turn, Jim would walk over the target marbles, hoping that a few would stick to the clay and get counted in his total score! More renowned for his marbling prowess, Jim could smash a pint glass (hopefully his own) that was four feet away with one flick of his tolley.

ESSENTIALS

The contest is played in a knockout format, with the first team to 25 points winning the match (except for the preliminary round, where the match ends after every player has taken four shots – even if 25 points has not been reached). Apart from keeping one knuckle in contact with the ground, cabbaging (shooting from the wrong spot) and fudging (moving the hand forward during the flick) are the other main rules to forget, should the referee ever have his back turned from the game!

Entry is normally by invitation only, but any new teams should get in touch with the organisers in advance to secure a place. There are two practice rings (don't graze your knuckles!) for those last-minute refinements or, in the case of absolute novices, to avoid looking too hopeless. Players unable to get a team together for the championship should arrive before the start and put their names on the reserve list, just in case any teams are short of players. Who knows, you may end up in a team with five complete strangers and win the contest!

Alongside the team event, there's also an individual marbles contest, which involves the defending champion plus each team's highest scorer from the first round – so even if the rest of the team stink, better players get another shot at glory. There are further prizes for the best lady competitor and the best golden oldie (over 50 years old), and even a trophy for players who have never won a game. In fact, it will be difficult to leave the contest without a prize! There's a cup for the team winners, and the runners-up receive beer. Many years ago, the runners-up prize was a barrel of beer, and there were suspicions that some teams threw away the final so that they could walk away with the far more appealing second prize!

TIPS

A strong thumb, good hand-eye coordination and nerves of steel are the usual responses from competitors prompted for advice. A total beginner can quickly pick up the basic technique and knock a few marbles off, but the best teams have been playing for decades. The key is to keep the tolley on the ring as long as possible, which means using plenty of spin. Beginners should keep it simple, though, aiming for marbles closest to the edge of the ring, with more chance of a successful hit, and not thinking too much about the next shot.

Jim Longhurst recommended constantly flicking the thumb to keep it strong, and the advice of four-times World Champion, Barry Ray, is 'to switch drinking hands, to prevent an extra chilled pint of lager freezing your thumb'. It's not considered *de rigueur* to wear a glove, but it acts as a great hand-warmer in between matches. While drinking and playing marbles go hand in hand, competitors should pace themselves, otherwise they may find it's not just the marbles that spin around! Another tip from the Atomic Thumb is to roughen up the tolley with a brick for better grip, but don't carry the brick around at the contest, or the opposition may get the wrong idea.

WACKY FACT

In the early days, Wee Willie Wright stuffed a hot water bottle inside his coat to keep his thumb warm between matches. It's not known whether he also tucked in a couple of pillows for a tactical nap.

IF YOU LIKE THIS

Good Friday is certainly a good day to be a marbles fanatic in Sussex, with another annual competition at Winkle Island, Hastings. The game takes place to remember the story of the Romans casting lots for Jesus Christ's clothes, with a re-enactment of the story earlier in the day. There's also the Battle Abbey Green Marbles Match, where over 100 teams take part, many turning up in weird fancy dress.

There's another World Marbles Championship, held in Prague in the Czech Republic, that has been going since 2005 and claims to be the World Championship at individual marbles. Meanwhile, the World Marbles on Sand Championship takes place in France, with national champions from 60 countries represented.

MATLOCK
RAFT RACE

'A festive race with a weir'ly nasty ending'

Location:	Matlock, Derbyshire
Date:	Boxing Day
Time:	From 10am
Entry fee:	£12 per crew member
Further information:	www.dasac.co.uk
Grid reference:	SK 297 601

Spectator Fun:	★★★
Wackiness:	★
Pain Factor:	★★★
Training Required:	★★★
Family Friendly:	★★★

WHAT HAPPENS

The definition of a raft is 'a flat buoyant structure of timber or other materials fastened together, used as a boat or floating platform' (*The New Oxford Dictionary of English* – Oxford Press, 1998). Luckily for the crowds watching the race, some of the teams neglected to read up on the definition of what a raft should look like, and probably had a daft race instead of a raft race in mind when they conceived their entries.

The four-mile raft race along the River Derwent, from Cawdor Quarry through the town of Matlock to Cromford Meadows, begins with the racing rafts, followed at a more leisurely pace by the comedy entries. Teams, which must include members of diving clubs, are dressed appropriately in wetsuits in anticipation of a trip into the water. Even if they can avoid a premature capsizing, they will still need to surmount the notorious weir towards the end.

Eagle-eyed officials scrutinise the rafts for riverworthiness as teams ponder their first test: how to transport the raft down the riverbank into the water using the very steep makeshift scaffold launch while hopefully remaining afloat, and without getting their hair wet or ruining their make-up!

This early challenge sifts out any weaker craft, which inevitably disintegrate on contact with the icy-cold river, much to the delight of the crowd, leaving the team to lament their premature demise and direct blame at whoever was responsible for the rope-knotting (and perhaps wishing they had entered the submarine category). A perfect example of what not to enter into the race was one team's outlandish idea of creating a large hamster wheel in the mistaken belief that it would literally walk on water – but before they could say 'Titanic', the raft sank.

Once safely in the water and afloat, those on the faster rafts (consisting of big plastic barrels) effortlessly paddle downstream. Unfortunately for the over-elaborate designs such as Viking ships, fire engines and dragons, less attention has been paid to streamlining and speed, resulting in many entries losing all volition and drifting from side to side, colliding with competing rafts, ramming into the bank or striking the pillar of one of several bridges. The only consolation for these teams is that no matter what happens, the rafts can only go one way eventually.

If abysmal steering wasn't enough of a handicap, trees frequently block the bridges, requiring the rafts to slot through half an arch. Two or more attempts are often required for the less coordinated or for those still under the weather from too much food and drink on Christmas Day. Teams with more fragile builds can only hope the raft sinks before they reach the event's *pièce de résistance* further down the course.

Spectators and participants interact along the course, with some rafts carrying on-board hosepipes, soaking unsuspecting onlookers lining the bank. The crowd get the opportunity to strike back, many loitering mischievously, ready to launch powdery missiles as the rafts pass by. Bridges are the favourite location for a spot of target practice, as rafts become sitting ducks for a barrage of flour bombs, the teams emerging on the other side completely whitewashed.

Unbeknown to the spectators, some teams have sneakily armed themselves too, paddling intentionally close to the riverbank to engage in an attack with their own culinary weaponry. Occasionally these exchanges become so intense that a team's steering becomes wayward, the raft getting grounded or entangled in tree branches, much to the delight of the crowd who can then launch a full-blown floury onslaught.

Besides the missiles, there are other hazards for the teams to consider, including half-submerged rocks and dumped shopping trolleys, none of which compare to the enormity of the task facing the teams as they approach Masson Mill. Here the river is dissected by a weir, with a fall of around 30 feet, and beyond this a section of rocks and tree trunks. Negotiating this part of the course will require some, if not all, of the team dismounting from the raft ... usually involuntarily.

As the rafts slow down on approaching the weir, the more experienced teams turn around to hit it sideways-on and walk the raft over the weir, to the dismay of the onlookers expecting plenty of capsizes.

For every raft manoeuvred with due care and attention, there are always a small number of teams not giving a damn, hitting the weir head-on. The lucky ones somehow manage to

stay upright and bounce along the rocks, coming to a rest in the calmer waters at the bottom. The less fortunate only partially clear the weir, leading to the amusing sight of a bed or a car pivoting precariously on the edge, those on board sliding into the water and soon finding themselves up the creek without a paddle or even a boat! The raft eventually drops down and everyone climbs back on, very red-faced.

Even after surviving the drop intact, teams must still negotiate a second, shorter plunge, which some tackle with too much confidence, causing the raft to flip over. Fortunately, safety crews surround the weir to rescue anyone unable to scramble back onto their raft.

Competitors then paddle, or drift, along the final stretch of calm water, dodging a few more flour bombs, before mustering enough energy for the exit out of the river, which involves ascending the bank, together with the raft, for an official finish. For the more flamboyant entries, this may simply require chucking a couple of barrels and planks onto the bank, along with whatever else may remain of their craft. The quicker rafts usually complete the course in around the one-hour mark, but comedy rafts can expect to take up to three hours.

HISTORY

The race is organised by the local diving clubs in Derbyshire to raise funds for the RNLI and has been going since 1963, with only one interruption when the river was too high. Around 40 rafts make the start every year, but not all get to the finish. The 200th anniversary of the Battle of Trafalgar saw the race appropriately won by HMS *Victory*. Among the more unusual entries seen in the race, there has been a boxing ring built on a wooden platform which successfully navigated the course, and another raft carried canons, one firing blanks and the other shooting out water.

ESSENTIALS

For safety reasons, there are several rules for each team to observe. Half of the crew must be members of a nationally accredited diving club, and everyone has to wear a suitable wet- or dry-suit and of course be able to swim, as capsizing is extremely likely. The minimum age for competitors is sixteen years, and there are no limits on the number of competitors on a single raft, but it will not be a case of the more the merrier. Teams can enter on the day, but obviously will need to start building their raft a few weeks before.

The crowd happily lob flour bombs but there has been a crackdown on eggs, with signs along the course warning everyone that 'missiles must not be thrown', erected after there was a serious eye injury a few years ago from a misdirected hard-boiled egg. Some competitors even wear eye shields just in case a similar incident happens again. Officials search all rafters for hidden supplies before they start, but those with a propensity for throwing eggs should instead enter the World Egg Throwing Championships (see page 196). Unsurprisingly, teams must not set off flares, unless they find themselves lost and requiring rescue! The winner receives a cup and plaque. The rest of the teams are probably thankful for finishing.

Spectators can view the race at most places along the course, with the A6 road running parallel to the river. Matlock Bridge is a popular venue early on, while the Parade in Matlock Bath is where the biggest crowds gather for the best view of the rafts and the messiest flour fights. Masson Mill towards the end of the course is the spot to head for if you are hoping to witness examples of calamitous rafting. There's free parking at the finish, at Cromford Meadows.

(TIPS)

Teams aiming to win the race should ensure that their raft has a solid base and is very buoyant, with plenty of clearance underneath. The river isn't always deep, and rafts with a keel will come unstuck as it snags on a rock or branch. Plastic barrels tied together or rubber inner tubes are sure-fire ways to speed down the river, with fitter teams even using paddles for additional propulsion. Don't forget to add some extra support when building the raft to account for the sudden gain in weight caused by all the team members!

For the less sturdy rafts, it's better to walk the raft around the weir rather than leaving your fate to the fast-flowing water, which inevitably sends a few entries into dire straits. The water will be very cold, and if you do finish the race wet, ensure that you change into dry clothing very quickly. Should the unthinkable happen and you fall into the river, swim to the riverbank, rejoining your team at a safe point.

WACKY FACT

One year, a team completed the course in an open canoe while cooking a barbeque on board. Along the way, they even sold soggy burgers to the crowd.

IF YOU LIKE THIS

There are mad raft races all over the UK, many with their own unique rules and requirements and all organised for charity. Just a few of these include the Wellesbourne & District and Shakespeare Lions Charity Raft Race, near Stratford, which runs seven miles along the River Avon and includes two weirs, the Rother Raft Race in Sussex, where teams must descend a

'Fish Ladder', and the Minehead Raft Race in Somerset, which hosts the biggest sea raft race in Britain.

The Mapleton Bridge Jump near Matlock (see page 158) also involves a chilly raft race on New Year's Day, but has the added pleasure of a splash into the river ... without the aid of a dry-suit!

UK NATIONAL SANDCASTLE COMPETITION

'Sun, surf, sea and stupendous sandcastles'

Location: Woolacombe, North Devon

Date: A Sunday in late June

Time: Midday

Entry fee: £75 per team

Further information:
www.northdevonhospice.org.uk

Grid reference: SS 456 438

Spectator Fun: ★★

Wackiness: ★

Training Required: ★★★

Family Friendly: ★★★★

---------(**WHAT HAPPENS**)----------

Arguably the most sedate event in the wacky calendar – until the sea starts getting closer and closer, that is.

No time for sunbathing as teams of six 'sandcastlers', dressed in shorts, sandals and the *de rigueur* handkerchief, descend on Woolacombe beach with buckets of energy, ready to show the kids up at their own game. Teams compete to build the most spectacular and artistic sand sculpture ... just don't expect to see too many castles with union jacks, which are far too passé.

Besides the obligatory buckets and spades, teams arrive well-prepared with an array of tools including trowels, watering cans, plumb lines, rakes, ice-cream scoops and copious sun cream; in fact, everything except the garden shed! In the expectation of plenty of hard work and hot weather, experienced teams prudently bring along a gazebo to ward off the sunburn – although a few years ago, the contest began in wall-to-wall sunshine, but after the sandcastles were completed the weather deteriorated to a downpour and the whole crowd ran off, leaving no one to admire the finished sculptures.

Teams take over their allocated seven-metre-square plot, with not a deck chair in sight. The team captain, who is the creative force, clutches the clandestine blueprint and discusses the final tactics and responsibilities. There is the Chief Bucket, two or three sculptors/diggers and the much-needed slave, aka the Chief Gopher. There needs to be an equal measure of brains and brawn among the team – too much muscle creates nothing more than a mound of sand to display, but an overdose on creativity will leave the entry up to the imagination.

One of the main rules of the contest restricts teams to sand from their own plot only, so the competition kicks off with frenetic excavations to create the foundations and stockpile the sand necessary for the sculpture. The Captain, meanwhile, bellows instructions at the diggers, ordering the Gopher off to the sea for the first of many tiring trips fetching buckets of water.

With a pile of sand in the middle of the plot, water is slowly mixed and then the hard work of pummelling and pounding the sand into the desired shape begins. The perfect formula for building sandcastles is roughly one part water to eight parts sand, and teams will soon realise if the ratio has gone to pot when the sculpture starts to blow away, or collapses into sludge. With the physically demanding stage complete, the artists in the team take the limelight, painstakingly carving and shaping the sand into recognisable features such as a turtle's head or a mermaid's tail.

Halfway through the contest, the Captain compares the design on paper to the reality, twisting his head this way and that until satisfied that the sculpture bears some resemblance to what it should actually look like, at least from one angle. There will, of course, always be the odd derisory comment aimed at the carvers, such as 'Are you sure that's where the tail should be?', or 'Why has the crocodile got a horse's head?' The tempo picks up as teams fall behind in their schedule and resort to dragging kids into the plot to muck in with the digging, while other teams regret not sneaking some quicksand into the competition to speed things up!

Those without the luxury of a gazebo worriedly eye the sun, which is now at its strongest, and bring out the watering can to moisten the sand and their foreheads. Competitors continue to display patience as the sand imperceptibly meta-morphoses into a seal or the back end of a Volkswagen Beetle (or is it a Ford Escort?).

With the sands of time running out, teams make some final touches to their masterpieces, with powdered paint or flour adding some colour to the entries. Teams can also use raw beach materials to enhance the design – which the now 'pail'-looking Gopher must retrieve – such as driftwood, sea-weed or pebbles. Even an empty beer can adds amusement to an entry when placed in the hand of a mermaid. Shopping trolleys, boat wreckage or old boots may not be so appropri-ate. Teams with any energy left clean up their entries, fussily smoothing out any rough edges or having one last-ditch attempt at digging a moat around their sculptures.

Officials end the contest, reminding the teams to down tools. Grudgingly everyone stands back to admire the sculp-tures (or pick out flaws), while firmly keeping one eye on the

encroaching tide and any wind-blown deck chairs heading in their direction – except the Gopher, that is, who collapses in exhaustion.

Originally, the spectators donated money to vote for the winning entry. Unfortunately, this tempted the more competitive teams to buy their win. Now, a local celebrity has the responsibility for deciding the winner. Later in the day, the teams must tearfully watch their ingenuity and graft wash away as the sea finally creeps over the sandcastles – that's if children don't get to the sculptures first!

HISTORY

The competition first started in 2001, with an enforced break in 2007 due to severe storms. Innovative recreations have ranged from polar bears to crocodiles to UFOs. There has even been a whale with Jonah's bottom and legs sticking out of its mouth. The biggest sculpture to date has been a five-foot panda, and another popular entry was a pirate ship that let off smoke pellets. The same team also blended a boy into the design, who surprised the judges by moving when they got too close.

Some entries don't finish as intended. The contest founders and current organisers, North Devon Hospice, usually enter it themselves, and once fashioned a strawberries-and-cream sculpture, only for a passer-by to admire their attempt and declare: 'What a lovely volcano!'

Teams should also have a back-up plan in case of pear-shaped eventualities, such as a misdirected football or frisbee smashing into the sculpture. One year, a team was working on a giant teddy bear when disaster struck, but some quick think-ing turned what remained into a small gorilla.

In 2006, organisers laid on a separate event to set an unof-ficial record for the longest line of sandcastles along the shoreline. This is likely to become a regular side attraction in future to keep the crowds occupied. Unfortunately, the world record for the longest sand sculpture spans over sixteen miles, which poses a dilemma for the three-mile-long beach at Woolacombe!

ESSENTIALS

The list of tools to bring along is limitless, but at a minimum, teams should have some of the following: long-handled shov-els, buckets, tools for carving, smoothing, scooping, etching and shaping (e.g. pastry knife, paint scraper), plus those handy implements (e.g. paintbrush, drinking straw, feather duster) to add the finishing touches. Don't forget a first aid kit to treat those blisters, and be careful not to bring along anything that's too dangerous-looking – this is a beach, not a building site.

JCBs and cement are definitely not permitted, although one year a competitor did ask if he could bring a digger along. Teams can also apply some environmentally friendly powdered paint to add a touch of colour, or just opt for *au naturel.*

The winning team collects the fabulous UK National Sand-castle Builders' Trophy, donated by Dartington Crystal. Team members must be over the age of sixteen, so younger children will have to wait until afterwards to bury their dads, but a helping hand from a keen youngster is not discouraged, if there's room in the plot.

(TIPS)

Ideas need to be very imaginative, but not too ambitious, as teams have only three hours' building time. Obviously, topical entries will be more popular, as proven by the three lions entry in 2006 to coincide with the football World Cup. Animals, fish and transport are recurring themes every year, but to really impress the judges come along with something completely original.

According to Suzanne Altamare, World Champion and Grandmaster Sand Sculptor, teams should 'keep stepping back from the sculpture and looking at it from where the crowd will see it, or maybe viewing it on a digital camera. You'll see any mistakes that way.' Organisation is the key, and Suzanne recommends that teams include somebody good with proportions to rough out the shapes, and others who are good at detail.

There's further advice from Lucinda 'Sandy Feet' Wierenga, author of the sandcastle bible, *Sandcastles Made Simple*: 'Most novice sand-sculptors would be amazed to discover how adding lots more water improves the carvability of the sand. Try digging down to the water table to extract extremely wet sand from the bottom of the hole and using that to create your structures. This way you won't have to carry so many buckets up from the shoreline.'

WACKY FACT

The world's tallest sandcastle stood at fifteen metres and was built in 2007 on Myrtle Beach, South Carolina. It took ten days to construct and required over 300 truckloads of sand. The USA also holds the record for the longest-standing sand sculpture, which lasted around two years in California.

IF YOU LIKE THIS

Sandcastle competitions are held all over the UK, and other recommended beaches to practice building sandcastles can be found in Tenby, Bournemouth, Bridlington – and not forgetting Blackpool.

The Sand Sculpture Festival, a Dutch conception, visits a different British resort every year. Over 60 international sculptors take about one month to create their own awesome 'sandmark', and in recent years Brighton, Great Yarmouth and Torbay have hosted the festival. There are over 150 sculptures, ranging from less than one metre in height up to an incredible ten metres.

For very patient sandcastlers only, Cromer in Norfolk hosts the annual Tide Fights every August. It's a case of last castle standing as competitors construct massive sandcastles and then nervously watch as the tide rolls in. One by one the sculptures collapse, until the final castle defiantly stands up to the sea and is declared the winner.

EGG ROLLING

'Don't eat all your eggs too soon!'

Location: Avenham Park,
Preston, Lancashire

Date: Easter Monday

Time: 10am until late afternoon

Entry fee: Free

Further information: www.preston.gov.uk;
Preston Tourist Information,
01772 253731

Grid reference: SD 537 288

Spectator Fun: ★★

Wackiness: ★

Pain Factor: ★★

Training Required: ★

Family Friendly: ★★★★★

─────────────(**WHAT HAPPENS**)─────────────

Children have a rollicking good time as they finally get the chance to eat their Easter eggs, just as long as they can break the shell first!

Continuing a custom going back to the Victorian era, hundreds of families head to Avenham Park and participate in the biggest mass egg roll in Britain. As a sign of the times, children no longer feel the need to gather hard-boiled eggs from around the neighbourhood before diligently dyeing them myriad colours. These days it's either a quick trip to the shop or an expectant wait on Easter Sunday for a visit from the Easter Bunny, as chocolate eggs outnumber the more traditional variety.

Standing on the edge of the bow-shaped hill, children clutch their chocolate eggs, some still hastily unwrapping the packaging, much to the chagrin of the token purists who stand patiently with their hard-boiled eggs. Seconds before the official roll, over-enthusiastic participants false-start, flinging their eggs down the short and steep grassy slope. The rest of the eggs soon follow, some limply dropped and rolling only a few yards, or becoming wedged in a hole. Other eggs are chucked with much more gusto, and children then begin a haphazard pursuit, slipping and sliding as they struggle to keep up with the pace of the egg. Behind the children, parents and grandparents are hot on their heels, poised to cushion the fall of any child suffering a mishap; but who will catch the adults when they fall?

Ostensibly, children compete to see whose egg rolls the furthest. They glance across the hillside, and if they find that their egg isn't in the lead, they apply one or two less-than-

subtle kicks to the egg to maintain its momentum. Not surprisingly, for those bringing along chocolate Easter eggs, the *raison d'être* for rolling is to eat the eggs, and there's an unwritten rule forbidding any scoffing until the shell has broken … legitimately. After the first roll, the majority of children disappointedly find the shell still intact and trundle back up the hill to try again.

Children repeat the roll several times, each time their brows increasingly furrowed as the egg refuses to surrender to the hill. The younger and less steady participants often land on their backsides as they give chase, but the lure of possible chocolate sees them recover quickly, keeping fingers crossed for a lucky break. In fact, the spectacle of hordes of tiring children running down the hill bears more than a passing resemblance to a beginner's version of the cheese rolling tradition (see page 186), but don't worry, the only thing cracking here will be the eggs!

Inevitably, the thought of the chocolate accelerates a child's desire to break the shell and they resort to some under-handed tactics to finish the job. A lob or firm kick sends the egg flying down the hill, watched in alarm by families who have set up picnics in the middle. The children pursue the egg optimistically, checking for irreparable damage and asking, 'Daddy, the egg's smashed, can I eat it now?' Lazier children realise that traipsing up and down the hill can be quite exhausting work, and partner up with a friend who stands at the bottom, although this alliance relies on the partner not running off to scoff the egg on their own!

As for those utterly resilient eggs, children end up slamming them into an unsuspecting parent's thigh, or failing that, giving them a strong stamp to inflict the *coup de grâce*. As the eggs run out towards the end of the day, children continue the tradition by rolling themselves down the hill.

HISTORY

From time immemorial, the tradition has symbolised the rolling away of the rock from the entrance to Jesus' tomb at the time of his resurrection. Fortunately, for those standing at the bottom of the hill, it was eggs and not rocks that became the chosen projectiles! Historically, egg rolling was exclusive to northern Britain. Arthur's Seat in Edinburgh, Bunker Hill in Derbyshire and the castle moat in Penrith, Cumbria were all at one time popular venues, but the tradition has since waned, mainly through the advent of chocolate eggs and alternative secular entertainment.

Eggs have rolled at Avenham Park for around 150 years (1862 is the earliest known record), and even today this venue remains the Mecca of egg rollers. In the early 20th century, women dressed up in Easter bonnets and children arrived with lattice baskets of eggs, all coloured using various natural dyes. Onion skins, beetroot and even spinach were popular choices, much to the relief of the children, who for one week a year had an excuse not to eat up all their vegetables!

With upwards of 40,000 people taking part in the tradition in its heyday, smarter children would often leave their hard-boiled eggs in a teapot of strongly brewed tea, before scratching their names on the shell, guaranteeing that they would retrieve the right egg at the bottom. Oranges, coconuts and even rubber balls were also rolled down the hill – hopefully the latter were never eaten! After the egg rolling, dancing and games took over until darkness ended the festivities. Today, the numbers have dwindled to the low thousands and only a small number of people make any concession to fancy dress, but the event is nevertheless a jovial affair.

In the old days, children would also participate in competitive jousts, rolling their egg at an opponent's egg until one of them broke. The competitive side to see who has the sturdiest egg has since lessened, with more incentive for breaking the egg to eat the chocolate – which is, after all, a lot more appealing than an egg tasting of onions!

Easter in Preston hasn't always been so light-hearted. In the 18th century, the town hosted the custom of bull-baiting (dogs attacking a tethered bull), but this ended in 1726 due to fighting between soldiers and townsfolk as they gambled and drank heavily.

ESSENTIALS

The egg rolling is the high point of a day-long festival of live music, Easter bonnet competitions, funfair rides and craft workshops. It's also one of the first opportunities in spring to enjoy the picturesque surroundings of the park – although an unseasonal snow shower interrupted the 2008 event, threatening to turn the egg rolling into a snowball fight. There's also talk that the 2009 egg roll may incorporate an official race.

There are three official mass egg rolls during the day, with further spontaneous rolls in between for impatient children and adults. Unless you are the beneficiary of an over-generous Easter Bunny, there are shops five minutes away for anyone desperate enough to have just one more roll.

TIPS

Don't roll too hard, otherwise the egg may find its way into the river at the bottom of the hill, and while not in the true spirit of the custom, chocolate eggs should be wrapped in a sealed bag if intended to be eaten at the end without added grass or dirt. Children should also pay heed to a Lancastrian legend – the eggshells need to be very carefully crushed, otherwise witches will steal the shell, turning it into a boat and sailing away (though the speed at which children devour the chocolate won't leave much time for the witches anyway).

Dogs are welcome in the park, but unless you want a mangled and half-bitten egg, put the dog on a lead while the egg is rolled. Finally, bring along some head protection, as children inevitably turn the event into an egg-throwing spectacle!

WACKY FACT

The White House in America hosts an egg rolling race every Easter Monday, but without a hill. Thousands of children use giant spoons to push the eggs along, in what must be the President's toughest engagement of his tenure. The tradition began in 1814 in the grounds of the US Capitol, and moved to the White House after complaints from the gardeners.

IF YOU LIKE THIS

Traditional egg rolling events now take place all over Britain, often following a short church service. Another famous roll takes place on Holcombe Hill, near Bury, but here, people simply climb to the top and then roll the egg back down. Be on your guard for eggs heading in the opposite direction as you ascend the hill. There's probably an egg roll in a village near you … that's the custom, not the sandwich!

Wackier egg rolls with a competitive element for those children (and adults) wishing to demonstrate their eggs-pertise have sprung up in the last few years. Soar Mill Cove near Salcombe is the venue for the World Egg Rolling

Championship. There's also an egg pitch-and-putt, an egg hunt, and even an egg catching competition – but watch out, as the latter doesn't involve hard-boiling the eggs beforehand. There are other notable egg rolling contests at Devil's Dyke in Sussex, Oadby in Leicestershire and Woolton Woods, Liverpool.

Shotover Country Park, near Oxford, hosts an egg-rolling contest with a difference. Besides prizes for the best painted egg and the fastest egg, there's also the unique Demolition Derby. Hard-boiled eggs are repeatedly rolled down the twenty-metre hill until there's one egg left intact – this is one contest where competitors and eggs mustn't crack under pressure.

CHRISTMAS PUDDING RACE

'After 27 years, the proof of the pudding
is still in the racing!'
Stephen Melchek of Cancer Research

Location: West Piazza, Covent Garden, London

Date: Second Saturday in December

Time: 11am

Entry fee: £500 per team (plus sponsorship)

Further information: www.cancerresearchuk.org and www.xmaspuddingrace.org.uk

Grid reference: TQ 303 808

Spectator Fun: ★★★★

Wackiness: ★★★

Pain Factor: ★

Training Required: ★

Family Friendly: ★★★★

WHAT HAPPENS

Pudding faces are the order of the day, but competitors needn't worry about piling on the fat around their cheeks – it's the Christmas puddings that are given a facelift.

A festive *It's a Knockout*-style madcap race hits Covent Garden, pitting teams of six against an assortment of devilish and tricky obstacles over a 150-metre course, all in the name of charity. Fortunately, there isn't any mistletoe to tackle!

The first competitors line up at the start, decked out in a wacky assortment of costumes. Wombles, nuns, Christmas crackers, reindeer and even a team of mad scientists clutch their Christmas puddings (the white sauce is added later on!), complete with a sprig of holly, ready to run the gauntlet. One member from each team completes the course twice, picking up half their team on each lap. In a further twist, competitors must transform their puddings into Mr Potato Heads, without dropping or crushing the pudding along the way.

While balancing the tray in one hand, entrants fly through a washing line of tea towels before diving into a barrel for a Christmas cracker, which is pulled with a team-mate, with groans from the crowd when they hear the awful joke. There's then a mad dash under the limbo balloons, and with no time to catch their breath, competitors find themselves entering the Mr Potato Head obstacle.

Sandwiched between several awkward-looking inflatable objects (don't wear tight trousers!) there are buckets containing the facial features required to build up the face, and competitors must attach them all securely and, more importantly, in the right place. Many competitors whizz past the buckets before hastily backtracking to pick up a nose.

Completing the course missing an eye or mouth will mean disqualification, as will bite-sized chunks taken out of the puddings, so don't enter the race on an empty stomach!

Having finished the face, runners then reach the highlight of the course – the inflatable slide. Clambering to the top, with plenty of friendly barging along the way, the aim is to descend the slide without launching the pudding into the crowd or ending up flat on your face. For those who sensibly wiggle down, the pudding remains intact, but for no 'rum or raisin' a few end up sliding down head-first, arms outstretched, hopelessly losing control of their tray and the pudding. Inevitably, there are some comical pile-ups between over-zealous competitors struggling to multi-task and coordinate themselves in their cumbersome fancy dress – expect to see mad wombles and antler-clad nuns crossing the finishing line minutes later!

After a quick test of their eyesight (sticking a bauble in the right place on a Christmas tree), competitors head on to the finale, where they encounter the white sauce topping. Officials lurk at the sidelines spraying jets of white foam at the puddings, though usually aiming waywardly, so watch out! Steamed-up competitors then plough through a wall of flour-filled balloons, using the sprig of holly to pop one of them, before coming out the other side as white as the Ghost of Christmas Past, slipping, sliding and stumbling towards the finishing line.

The first person from each team over the finishing line must now hurtle around the course once again, picking up the rest of their team and bringing back their own two-faced pudding. Before announcing the winners, judges scrutinise the puddings for face defects – that is, if anything remains left on the tray. Luckily for the competitors, and the crowd who are keen to get off to do some Christmas shopping, the officials don't expect the puddings to be presented with flaming brandy – otherwise everyone could be there all day waiting for the puddings to be set alight!

HISTORY

When Covent Garden re-opened in 1980 as a tourist attraction, the Cancer Research Aid Committee was asked to provide a focal point and lay on some imaginative entertainment. Their first event was a big success and they have been organising the festive race ever since, which raises around £15,000 every year for cancer research.

The race was originally around the perimeter of Covent Garden, but has since been restricted to a smaller area in the West Piazza, which has not detracted from the extremely friendly atmosphere.

Fancy dress is a pre-requisite, and one team arrived as the nativity scene, causing a few problems for baby Jesus, struggling to get around the course in his crib! Another time a pantomime cow entered, but it had an 'udderly' terrible time negotiating the obstacles and was traumatised by the slide!

ESSENTIALS

There are three separate categories: corporate, university and youth. However, when there are insufficient numbers, the categories are combined. Should there be any dead heats, then a face-off will determine the winner! Winning teams receive the prestigious Christmas Pudding Trophy as well as wine, games and food – plus a slightly mangled pudding if they're peckish. Teams should apply to enter the race as soon as possible, with a maximum of twelve teams per race, although individuals can enter (for a £100 donation) on the day and join in, if a team has space available. Every year organisers add a new obstacle to the course, hoping to baffle even the most experienced competitor or pantomime cow.

TIPS

Balance and speed are crucial, but choose your fancy dress wisely. Then again, the funnier the costume, the more money that will be raised for Cancer Research, so make the effort. You could even dress up as a giant Christmas pudding, although you would probably need a very big tray! Even if you can't manage a full costume, at least get into the spirit of things and wear a Christmas hat. Finally, if you find yourself in a battle with a pantomime cow to reach the inflatable slide … let the cow go down first!

WACKY FACT

One competitor wasn't kidding a few years ago when a goat was brought along for company during the race. No prizes for guessing what happened to all the Christmas puddings at the end.

IF YOU LIKE THIS

2007 saw the inaugural Santa Olympics, held at Wookey Hole in Somerset (www.wookeyhole.co.uk). Phoney Santas will soon be exposed, as competitors battle it out over nine different disciplines, each one part and parcel of their main occupation, from demonstrating their 'Ho ho hos' to boot tossing, sack racing, and a mince pie and spoon race. There's even wheelbarrow pushing, testing those who have spent the year working on their belly too much. But there isn't yet a contest for the biggest beard or the quickest brandy drinker!

BRAMBLES CRICKET MATCH

'Absolutely batty!'

Location: Brambles Bank, The Solent. Halfway between Southampton and Cowes, Isle of Wight

Date: Mid- to late August (dependent on tides)

Time: Usually around sunrise

Entry fee: None

Further information: www.islandsc.org.uk and www.royal-southern.co.uk

Grid reference: 50° 47 41 N, 1° 17 15 W

Spectator Fun: ★★★★

Wackiness: ★★★★

Family Friendly: ★

WHAT HAPPENS

A game of cricket would normally end up in a book dedicated to slow, measured and soporific sports, but there's one exception to this rule due to a quirk of nature.

Once a year, Brambles Bank, a submerged sandbank in the middle of the Solent, fully emerges from the sea for about 30 minutes as the spring tide reaches its lowest point. Two yacht clubs – Royal Southern Yacht Club based in Hamble, and the Island Sailing Club on the Isle of Wight – take full advantage of this 'arena' to compete in a bizarre cricket match. Over the years, the bank was notorious for grounding sailing vessels, and the game of cricket is maybe one way in which the yachtsman can hit back at nature!

Before sunrise, a fleet of yachts and dinghies heads for the bank and drops anchor, patiently waiting for the pitch to slowly reveal itself – a mesmerising sight. As soon as the first stretch of sand is exposed, players and spectators wade through knee-high water (don't wear your best pair of whites) and scramble onto the bank with bat, ball and scoreboard. A few spectators decline to get their feet wet, preferring to view the action from their boat with a glass of champagne.

The bank is around 200 metres in length and just big enough to accommodate everyone and allow for a decent game … as long as there are no big hitters! Players face an early challenge to find somewhere dry to place the wickets, then with pleasantries curtailed, the teams toss up and the action starts immediately in what is probably the shortest game of cricket in history (and better for it). A further oddity of the match is that no matter who has the stronger team, the winner of this bizarre competition is decided beforehand.

So expect plenty of controversial scoring and illogical decisions from the umpire towards the end to avoid a rewriting of the script.

Dressed in muddy whites and wellington boots, cricket etiquette is relaxed in conditions where a sand wedge would be more appropriate than a cricket bat. Players take their positions, and from a spectator's viewpoint it appears that everyone is fielding at 'very silly mid-wicket'. Pity the player nominated to stand at 'deep extra cover'!

Early on, the players take the game half-seriously, striving for a semblance of normality – although the poor state of the pitch, with water covering the length of the wicket, severely hampers any decent bowling and batting. Fast bowlers take care not to start their run-up too far back and precariously pace towards the wicket, unleashing a powerful ball that anticlimactically finds its way into one of many deep pools of water. Should the ball make it all the way, the bounce (or lack of it) surprises the batsman and he can only lash out wildly.

Often the batsman advances, hoping to smack the ball on the volley before it lodges in the sand, but usually he misjudges the shot and is out for a duck! When contact is made, both batsmen attempt to run the length of the hazardous pitch, which more closely resembles an assault course. After a few overs of flippers, floaters and paddle sweeps with more howzats than hoorays, the game descends into chaos as the peculiar surroundings infect the players' focus and underhanded tactics begin to dominate. Opposition fielders restrain the batsman from behind to prevent a stroke being played, or rugby-tackle him into a puddle during a quick run.

At one point, the dog mascot streaks onto the pitch and pinches the ball, forcing both teams to set off in pursuit,

which, if possible, makes the whole proceedings even more comical. The dog eventually releases the ball and is banished to square leg. This is a very surreal contest, and an even more ridiculous sight for the passengers of the ferries that sail past, who rub their eyes in disbelief when they catch sight of cricketers walking on water. Ferry passengers may even have the opportunity to catch a six!

No sooner has the game got going than the waters return and begin to lap up over the sandbank, eyed suspiciously by the groundsman. The players hurriedly complete the final over with the capitulation of the 'losing' team from a winning position – with some help from the official scorer! After a quick photo-call for the winners, everybody dashes off towards their boats. The groundsman vainly attempts to keep the pitch dry, but eventually declares the game abandoned due to a waterlogged pitch.

Players and spectators sail off to the yacht club, skipping cucumber sandwiches for a champagne breakfast. With a fond farewell, the last footprints and lost balls succumb to the encroaching tide, and for another year the world's most temporary sporting arena is hidden under water. Hasn't anyone thought of playing under water? ... maybe the first-ever snorkelling cricket match – don't mention this to Gordon Green!

HISTORY

Boat designer, yachtsman and general eccentric Uffa Fox decided to stage a game of cricket on the bank back in the 1950s after marvelling at the feat of nature and wondering how it could be put to good use. The inaugural match was between Uffa's work crew and prison officers from the nearby Parkhurst Prison. Sadly, the prisoners were never invited to play on the Solent's equivalent of Alcatraz! Back in the old days, the games were played more seriously, and there was a law that sixes were given whenever the ball landed in water. Of course, this meant that whoever won the toss would study the tides to judge whether batting first or second would yield more boundaries. Uffa would even raise a red ensign and his racing flag, the skull and crossbones, for the duration of the game.

In subsequent years, Uffa managed to organise a hover-craft (they were built on the Isle of Wight) to transport the players to the bank, parking on one end of the sand, while there was an international feel to proceedings on another occasion, when England cricketer Colin Cowdrey was invited along. Even after he passed away, the memory of Uffa lived on through a bust which was often brought along by the teams to umpire the match.

Despite the limited time for the teams to play the match, a few years ago the players assembled a drinks bar on the bank when the game was played in the evening, complete with a sign proclaiming: 'Open once a year for one hour'. Unfortunately, it was too much to ask the players to bring the pool table and jukebox.

Finally, the bank is slowly moving westwards and one day may reach land. Sadly, the game will then no longer merit a mention in this book.

ESSENTIALS

The game is played exclusively between members of the two yacht clubs. Spectators can watch the match and may be able to hitch a lift on one of the yachts leaving Hamble or the Isle of Wight, but it's better to ring in advance. Alternatively, charter your own yacht – the bank is about twenty minutes' sailing from Hamble ... just don't drop anchor on the pitch itself.

TIPS

Spectators should head to the bank only if they are experienced sailors – the players would not appreciate having to abandon their match to rescue anybody. First-timers who arrive on their own yacht should be careful not to outstay their welcome on the bank. Over the years, many players and spectators have had narrow escapes as the tide turned unexpectedly quickly.

WACKY FACT

There was once an incongruous mentioning of this wacky tradition during a less-than-enthralling debate at the Houses of Parliament (and recorded in Hansard). A local MP discussed the Brambles Bank game in an attempt to prove a point regarding the licensing of events and responsibilities between authorities.

IF YOU LIKE THIS

A similar game takes place at Goodwin Sands off the Kent coast, and is contested on an annual basis by the local potholing club. Future matches were put in doubt when a BBC TV crew were rescued off the bank recently. For other sports in aquatic environments, there's Football in the River at Bourton-on-the-Water, Gloucestershire (see page 240) and Mountain Bike Bog Snorkelling in Llanwrtyd Wells, Wales (see page 261).

WORLD COAL CARRYING CHAMPIONSHIPS

'A chance to be King or Queen of the Coil Humpers!'

Location: Gawthorpe, near Osset, West Yorkshire, just off J40, M1. The Royal Oak pub is close to Dewsbury rugby ground

Date: Easter Monday

Time: Races begin about 11am, until 1pm

Entry fee: £5

Further information: www.gawthorpe.ndo.co.uk

Grid reference: SE 273 221

Spectator Fun: ★★

Wackiness: ★★

World Champion: ★★★

Pain Factor: ★★★

Training Required: ★★★★★

Family Friendly: ★★★

WHAT HAPPENS

A real test of speed, strength and idiocy as men and women race over a distance of just under one mile while carrying a sack of coal. To make things even tougher for the competitors, the race runs up a hill and in the opposite direction from the pub. Luckily, the wicked sense of humour of the officials doesn't extend to using red-hot pokers to speed the runners up.

The race begins at the Royal Oak pub, where competitors limber up or maybe have a few stiff drinks before facing their first challenge – picking the sack up: a 50kg sack for men, while the women have to contend only with a 20kg sack. For the men, lifting the sack off the ground is strenuous enough, and sensibly, the coal is loaded from the lorry straight on to the competitors' shoulders. Otherwise this could inadvertently become a weightlifting contest! Competitors are also reminded, no matter how heavy the going gets: 'whatever you do, do not drop the sack.'

Poised at the start line, with a hunched posture and a tight grip on the sack, competitors feel the strain of the coal even before the race has started. There is an absence of any 'fun' entries, and everyone taking part has credible intentions about winning. Short and stocky Lycra-clad competitors replace the usual array of skinny legs and fancy dress seen at most wacky events. Tree stumps for legs are ideal in this event. A few runners even wear back support belts, having entered one too many races over the years.

Not long into their stride and competitors reach the bottom of a long, steady hill climbing towards the village centre. Shoulders drop as they make their ascent, keeping their heads down to avoid eye contact with what lies ahead. Many of the entrants find the hill too much, and less than halfway along they feel their legs buckle, lungs explode and backs creak, as they are suddenly confronted with the enormity of the task, doubting their sanity for entering in the first place! Those lucky enough to manage the climb have a brief respite before hitting the home straight. Spurred on by the cash prize, they stubbornly edge nearer to the finish line while betraying their discomfort with tired grimaces and loud groans.

The sack of coal must be placed at the bottom of the May-pole for the competitor to officially finish, but just getting that far will be enough for most. Some of the fitter entrants will end the race with a quick burst of pace to demonstrate their strength and agility; others, however, will stagger over the line and collapse on top of their sack in sheer exhaustion.

There is always at least one competitor who finds the weight of the sack too much and stupidly drops it in the middle of the road – there is a reason why the competitors are assisted at the start! After several unsuccessful attempts to lift the sack on to their shoulders, they lose patience and hold it out in front, hobbling to the finish with gritted teeth. Luckily, the race is very well supported and the predominantly local competitors are furiously cheered on.

HISTORY

The idea was born back in 1962 when two local men, probably intoxicated at the time, had a wager on who was the more fit. There was a brief idea of staging a rolling-pin-throwing contest, until the men figured that women would have an advantage over them and turned their attention to a contest requiring raw power. The same year, the two men – one appropriately a coal miner – held battle, and the following year entries were open to anybody mad enough to join them.

The current world record is 4 minutes 6 seconds for the men and 4 minutes 48 seconds for the women, who have only been racing since 1995. Even without a coal sack, these times are impressive! The oldest-ever entrant was a 77-year-old who, despite his gallant efforts, failed to finish. There was no shame in this, as many men half his age often struggle to complete the course. In 2006 even the reigning world champion found himself tiring, stumbling near the finish line and being overtaken.

ESSENTIALS

There are only 30 entries available for each of the main races. About half of the entries are available on the day itself, but no later than 11am. A postal entry in advance is required to secure one of the other fifteen places. There are also three prizes in each race, with £300 and £100 going to the men's and women's winners respectively. Parking is available at the Royal Oak pub, but not anywhere along the route.

Before the main contest, there is a children's race involving a shorter distance and a lighter 10kg sack, enabling entrants to complete the course at a canter. Before spectators harbour ideas of taking part in the senior race, they should note that the coal for the children is made of polystyrene!

TIPS

50kg of coal is very heavy and just dragging the sack is cumbersome enough, so unless you are physically able, avoid entering. The sack should be placed comfortably resting across the shoulders and high up on the neck, gripping two corners of the sack very firmly. On no account drop the bag for a rest ... unless it's in resignation.

The best weight for a male competitor is around eleven stone, with farmers and window cleaners the more favoured occupations, although coal miners would probably have an advantage too. A former winner prepared for the race by training with a sack of potatoes.

IF YOU LIKE THIS

There's the Scottish Coal Carrying Championship, held in Kelty on the last Saturday in June. Inspired by the races in Gawthorpe, officials from Kelty took the idea north of the border and from 1995 coal carrying became part of the town's annual gala. The only differences are a shorter route, of 1,000 metres, and that the women have to carry 25kg instead of 20kg.

For a lighter load of only 60lb, try the Woolsack Race in Tetbury, Gloucestershire, held every Spring Bank Holiday Monday (see page 203). Be warned: to make up for the lighter weight, the hill is a lot steeper and the competitors are much quicker.

OTTERY ST MARY TAR BARRELS

'A barrel of laughs, as long as you keep your distance!'

Location:	Ottery St Mary, Devon. Off the A303 between Exeter and Honiton
Date:	5 November (when this falls on Sunday, it's held on Saturday)
Time:	Starts around 4pm and continues until midnight
Entry fee:	None, but a fee is charged to park
Further information:	www.otterytarbarrels.co.uk
Grid reference:	SY 099 954

Spectator Fun:	★★★★★
Wackiness:	★★★
Pain Factor:	★★
Family Friendly:	★★

WHAT HAPPENS

Local men and women hurtle around the streets of Ottery St Mary, carrying (called 'rolling') flaming barrels of tar on their backs. This is one event not for the faint-hearted, where being close up to the action adds to the excitement but will probably leave you in need of a good tonsorialist.

Held on Bonfire Night, the tradition probably goes back to the 18th or 19th century as a ritual for warding off evil spirits. Nowadays, barrel rollers and spectators let the spirits in to bolster confidence. A total of seventeen barrels are rolled throughout the evening, beginning with the boys' barrels, and later on the men and women take over the responsibility. The barrels, which can be as heavy as 100 kilograms, are coated in coal tar during the preceding months, and nearer to the day are stuffed with paper and straw to ensure that they are successfully set alight.

On the actual night, the barrels are distributed among the town's pubs, and from the first boys' barrel to the grand finale they are run one after the other. Local families sponsor each of the barrels in memory of a friend or relative, and the honour of running the barrel has often passed through many generations of the same family.

When a barrel arrives outside one of the pubs, the crowd draw closer in anticipation, watching as the rollers set alight the tar and eagerly awaiting the first flickers. As soon as the flames have taken, the crowd quickly lurch back as the first official roller hoists the barrel up on to their shoulders, probably with some assistance. After steadying the barrel they run up the street, gingerly at first, but after getting into their stride they move with less apprehension and more gusto.

With five-foot flames licking the sky, each run of the barrel brings about a massive surge in the crowd, and onlookers must dodge out of the way, or cower, as the barrel of flaming tar comes hurtling down the street straight at them. Sometimes, the crowd parts into two as the barrel roller steadfastly holds his position and cuts right through the middle, expecting everyone else to shift. The runner then returns and repeats the feat a second and third time, including some random surges. Frequently the barrel is rolled alongside a wall, and those standing in what seemed at first to be a safe spot will need to react quickly to the barrel to avoid walking home with singed eyebrows. The rollers occasionally interrupt their run with the odd flamboyant twirl, earning rapturous applause from the crowd, although this extra act in the proceedings has been toned down in recent years due to safety concerns.

Those closest to the action often scream, half in jest but also with genuine fear, as the barrel moves within scorching distance, each twist and turn of the barrel setting off yet another Mexican wave of pandemonium among the crowd. Signs are dotted around the town warning everyone that they are here at their own risk, and some of the less enthusiastic spectators probably wish they had paid heed to them now.

Apart from a pair of industrial-sized gloves and a towel to cushion the barrel (plus a hat for the women), there's minimal protection for rollers, and it often shows in the gritted teeth and puffed red cheeks, the adrenalin rush and pride from taking part pushing them through the pain barrier.

Without the over-enthusiastic crowd, the tradition would have little impact, but often the spectators become a hindrance as a combination of naivety and alcohol creates an extremely claustrophobic arena. Fortunately for the roller, his small team runs alongside the barrel to clear away any foolhardy spectators who figure it's macho to wait until the last minute to dive for cover. They are also on hand to guard against anyone who tries to tap the barrel, as any undue weight could cause it to fall into the crowd – though this has never yet happened. However, don't even think about toasting your marshmallows on the flames!

After a couple of laps, the roller swaps over to recover from the heat. Should the flames die down or the roller suddenly be overcome with exhaustion, the barrel will abruptly drop to the ground. The team gather round, and after a nervous moment for the crowd, the barrel is successfully re-ignited, and off it goes for an encore around the street. Inevitably, there's resignation among the crowd as the barrel drops for a final time and disintegrates, leaving behind a small pyre in the middle of the street. With a melancholic cheer, the crowd disperses, many racing on to the next barrel run.

As the evening proceeds, the barrels and rollers get steadily bigger, climaxing in the midnight barrel, which weighs about 120 kilos and stands at five feet tall. Not surprisingly, it requires two men to hoist it up. Everyone sings 'Auld Lang Syne' as the final barrel is prepared. After the last stubborn flames die away, the crowd head off home, their faces as black as the tar and their clothes in urgent need of washing.

HISTORY

Other than a ritual to cleanse the town of evil, the tradition could also refer to the fumigation of local shops using smouldering barrels in bygone times – or even be a celebration of the demise of Guy Fawkes.

Barrel rolling traditions were once a common sight throughout the country, but now Ottery St Mary is the sole remaining venue for this version of the barrel roll, attracting around 15,000 spectators. Incredibly, casualties are very rare, as both runners and spectators show respect for the tradition, although in a previous year one wall did collapse under the strain of the crowd. Locals have to earn the right to take part, which means participating from an early age and, after every year or so, rolling a bigger barrel (provided they grow quickly enough). Former residents of the town even make an annual pilgrimage from as far as Australia so that they can still be involved in the ritual.

The day traditionally begins with a small number of locals firing hand-held cannons at 5.30am. Further firing occurs in the afternoon as a prelude to the first of the barrels. 5 November is definitely not a day for sleeping in this town.

ESSENTIALS

The event is very well organised and everyone cooperates to ensure that the tradition continues unchanged. The boys begin proceedings at 4pm with the first of six barrels rolled. Then at 7.30 the men start rolling, with two ladies' barrels sandwiched in between the men's, at around 9pm. Each barrel run usually lasts for up to 30 minutes. Programmes are sold in the town, including a timetable and map showing the whereabouts of each barrel, essential for any newcomer.

Parking is a major issue, with the town closed off to cars from mid-afternoon until the last barrel has rolled. Police will tow away any car that's in the way, but a nearby field on the edge of Ottery St Mary is usually available for a small fee. The event includes a massive bonfire, fireworks display and funfair, should the tar barrels become too frightening.

TIPS

If you bring small children to the event or are concerned for your own safety, watch the earlier barrel runs at a safe distance before the crowds build up and then seek sanctuary in the pub. First-timers should follow similar advice to understand what happens, before plunging into the middle of the action 'with both barrels'.

For those still keen to be closer to the flames, it's advisable to get to one of the pubs well in advance. The main square allows the barrel rolling in a circular motion, and is therefore the ideal venue for spectators, while the other locations are situated along narrow streets and can feel very claustrophobic when everyone is crammed tightly to the wall. On the flip-side, at least in the narrow streets the barrel will only ever move in one of two directions.

WACKY FACT

Over 30 years ago, those taking part were permitted to drink cider before they carried the barrels. Unfortunately, in an age of high insurance costs, the drinking side of the tradition has been tamed, but this hasn't stopped the crowd from compensating for the rollers' sobriety.

IF YOU LIKE THIS

On the Saturday following Bonfire Night, Hatherleigh in West Devon also hosts a tar barrel run, but here the barrels are tied onto a sledge and pulled by around fifteen men at a frighteningly high speed through the town. Obviously, the evil spirits are a lot harder to get rid of in Hatherleigh. For insomniacs, they even have an earlier barrel run at 5am.

ENGLAND

North East

DURHAM
Seaburn Boxing Day Dip, Sunderland
World Jarping Championship

YORKSHIRE
Oxenhope Straw Race
The Great Knaresborough Bed Race
World Coal Carrying Championships
World Water Bombing Championships

LINCOLNSHIRE
Haxey Hood
World Egg Throwing Championships
World Russian Egg Roulette Championships

North West

CUMBRIA
Uppies and Downies
The World's Biggest Liar
World Gurning Championship

LANCASHIRE
Egg Rolling
Holcombe Hill Egg Rolling
Lancashire Waiters' Dash Championships
World Black Pudding Throwing Championships
World Clog Cobbing Championships

World Gravy Wrestling Championships
World Pie Eating Championship

CHESHIRE
Albert Dock Boxing Day Dip
Liverpool Egg Rolling Championships
Liverpool Santa Dash
World Worm Charming Championships

ISLE OF MAN
Peel New Year Dip
World Tin Bath Championships

Midlands

DERBYSHIRE
Bonsall World Championship Hen Races
Great Kinder Beer Barrel Challenge
Mapleton Bridge Jump
Matlock Raft Race
Royal Shrovetide Football Game, Ashbourne

NOTTINGHAMSHIRE
World's Greatest Liar

STAFFORDSHIRE
Lichfield Pancake Race

WEST MIDLANDS
Pantomime Horse Grand National

SHROPSHIRE
Sheep and Goat Grand Nationals
Waiters' (and Waitresses') Race
Wrekin Barrel Race

HEREFORDSHIRE
Wife Carrying Competition

LEICESTERSHIRE
Bottle Kicking and Hare Pie Scramble
Oadby Egg Rolling
Vale of Belvoir Conker Championships

WARWICKSHIRE
Atherstone Shrovetide Football Game
Wellesbourne & District and Shakespeare Lions Charity
    Raft Race

NORTHAMPTONSHIRE
World Conker Championships

East

NORFOLK
World Snail Racing Championships

SUFFOLK
British Open Crabbing Championship

CAMBRIDGESHIRE
Mascot Grand National
Stilton Cheese Rolling World Championships
World Pea Shooting Championships

ESSEX
Maldon Mud Race

South East

OXFORDSHIRE
Shotover Egg Rolling
The Great Shirt Race
World Pooh Sticks Championships

BUCKINGHAMSHIRE
Olney Pancake Race

MIDDLESEX
UK Mobile Phone Throwing Championships

LONDON
Christmas Pudding Race
Drag Olympics
Great Spitalfields Pancake Race
Peter Pan Cup Christmas Morning Handicap Swim

KENT
Edam Cheese Rolling, Ide Hill
Goodwin Sands Cricket
Three Horseshoes Wheelie Bin Race
World Custard Pie Throwing Championships
World Walking the Plank Championships

SURREY
National Egg Throwing Championships

SUSSEX
Battle Abbey Green Marbles Match
Brighton Christmas Day Swim
British and World Marbles Championship
Devil's Dyke Easter Egg Rolling

International Bognor Birdman
John Lidbetter All-Weather Open International Stone
    Skimming Competition
Rother Raft Race
Winkle Island Marbles
World Crazy Golf Championships
World Pea Throwing Championships

HAMPSHIRE
Brambles Cricket Match

South West

GLOUCESTERSHIRE
Cooper's Hill Cheese Rolling
Football in the River
Onion Eating Contest
Randwick Wap
Shin Kicking Championships (Cotswold Olympick Games)
Tetbury Woolsack Race

WILTSHIRE
Bradford-on-Avon Pancake Race

DORSET
Wimborne Minster Pancake Race
World Nettle Eating Championship

SOMERSET
Mince Pie Eating Contest
Minehead Raft Race
Santa Olympics

DEVON

Barum Santa Fun Run

Budleigh Salterton Christmas Day Swim

Exmouth Christmas Day Dip

Hatherleigh Tar Barrels

International Worm Charming Contest

Ottery St Mary Tar Barrels

Royal Marines Commando Challenge

Sheep Grand National

South West Birdman Competition

Swimbridge Wheelie Bin Race

Totnes Orange Races

UK National Sandcastle Competition

Waiters' and Waitresses' Race, Dartmouth

Waiters' and Waitresses' Races, Salcombe

World Egg Rolling Championship

CORNWALL

St Columb Hurling Match

JERSEY

Jersey Swimming Club Christmas Day Swim

SARK

Sark Sheep Races

NORTHERN IRELAND

COUNTY TYRONE

Northern Ireland Bog Snorkelling Championships

SCOTLAND

ANGUS
Haggis Hurling

ARGYLL AND BUTE
Swamp Soccer New World Championships
World Stone Skimming Championships

FIFE
Scottish Coal Carrying Championship, Kelty

LOTHIAN
Loony Dook

PERTHSHIRE
World Championship Haggis Eating Competition

WALES

CARMARTHENSHIRE
Welly Wanging, National Mud Festival
Walrus Dip

PEMBROKESHIRE
Wales Open Stone Skimming Championships

POWYS
Newtown Santa Race
Real Ale Ramble
Real Ale Wobble
World Bog Snorkelling Championships
World Bog Snorkelling Triathlon Championships
World Mountain Bike Bog Snorkelling Championships
World Mountain Bike Chariot Racing Championships

UNFIXED LOCATION

World Beard and Moustache Championships

World Sand Sculpture Festival

World Winter Swimming Championships

ABROAD

International Waiters' Race, Ghent, Belgium

World Marbles Championship, Prague, Czech Republic

World Marbles on Sand Championship, France

JANUARY
Haxey Hood
Mapleton Bridge Jump
Peel New Year Dip
World Mountain Bike Chariot Racing Championships

FEBRUARY
Atherstone Shrovetide Football Game
Bradford-on-Avon Pancake Race
Great Spitalfields Pancake Race
Lichfield Pancake Race
Olney Pancake Race
Royal Shrovetide Football Game, Ashbourne
St Columb Hurling Match
Wimborne Minster Pancake Race
World Winter Swimming Championships

MARCH
World Pooh Sticks Championships

APRIL
Battle Abbey Green Marbles Match
Bottle Kicking and Hare Pie Scramble
British and World Marbles Championship
Devil's Dyke Easter Egg Rolling
Egg Rolling
Haggis Hurling
Holcombe Hill Egg Rolling
International Worm Charming Contest

Liverpool Egg Rolling Championships
Oadby Egg Rolling
Sheep Grand National
Shotover Egg Rolling
Uppies and Downies
Winkle Island Marbles
World Clog Cobbing Championships
World Coal Carrying Championships
World Egg Rolling Championship
World Jarping Championship

MAY

Cooper's Hill Cheese Rolling
Edam Cheese Rolling, Ide Hill
Randwick Wap
Sheep and Goat Grand Nationals
Stilton Cheese Rolling World Championships
Tetbury Woolsack Race
The Great Shirt Race
World Water Bombing Championships
Wrekin Barrel Race

JUNE

Shin Kicking Championships (Cotswold Olympick Games)
Scottish Coal Carrying Championship, Kelty
Sheep and Goat Derby
Swamp Soccer New World Championships
The Great Knaresborough Bed Race
UK National Sandcastle Competition
Wellesbourne & District and Shakespeare Lions Charity
    Raft Race

World Custard Pie Throwing Championships
World Egg Throwing Championships
World Nettle Eating Championship
World Russian Egg Roulette Championships
World Tin Bath Championships
World Worm Charming Championships

JULY
Drag Olympics
Goodwin Sands Cricket
National Egg Throwing Championships
Northern Ireland Bog Snorkelling Championships
Oxenhope Straw Race
Sark Sheep Races
South West Birdman Competition
Three Horseshoes Wheelie Bin Race
World Bog Snorkelling Triathlon Championships
World Marbles Championship
World Mountain Bike Bog Snorkelling Championships
World Pea Shooting Championships
World Sand Sculpture Festival
World Snail Racing Championships

AUGUST
Bonsall World Championship Hen Races
Brambles Cricket Match
British Open Crabbing Championship
Football in the River
Gambo Race
John Lidbetter All-Weather Open International Stone
    Skimming Competition

Minehead Raft Race
Rother Raft Race
Totnes Orange Races
UK Mobile Phone Throwing Championships
Waiters' and Waitresses' Race, Dartmouth
Waiters' and Waitresses' Races, Salcombe
Wales Open Stone Skimming Championships
World Bog Snorkelling Championships
World Marbles on Sand Championship
World Championship Haggis Eating Competition
World Tin Bath Championships
World Walking the Plank Championships

SEPTEMBER

Great Kinder Beer Barrel Challenge
International Bognor Birdman
International Waiters' Race
Lancashire Waiters' Dash Championships
Onion Eating Contest
Waiters' (and Waitresses') Race, Ludlow
Welly Wanging, National Mud Festival
World Black Pudding Throwing Championships
World Gravy Wrestling Championships
World Gurning Championship
World Stone Skimming Championships

OCTOBER

Mascot Grand National
Royal Marines Commando Challenge
Vale of Belvoir Conker Championships
Wife Carrying Competition

World Conker Championships
World Crazy Golf Championships
World Pea Throwing Championships

NOVEMBER
Hatherleigh Tar Barrels
Mince Pie Eating Contest
Ottery St Mary Tar Barrels
Pantomime Horse Grand National
Real Ale Ramble
Real Ale Wobble
The World's Biggest Liar
World's Greatest Liar

DECEMBER
Albert Dock Boxing Day Dip
Barum Santa Fun Run
Brighton Christmas Day Swim
Budleigh Salterton Christmas Day Swim
Exmouth Christmas Day Dip
Christmas Pudding Race
Jersey Swimming Club Christmas Day Swim
Liverpool Santa Dash
Loony Dook
Maldon Mud Race
Matlock Raft Race
Mince Pie Eating Contest
Newtown Santa Race
Peter Pan Cup Christmas Morning Handicap Swim
Santa Olympics
Seaburn Boxing Day Dip, Sunderland

Swimbridge Wheelie Bin Race

Walrus Dip

World Pie Eating Championship

Iain Aitch, *A Fete Worse Than Death* (Review, 2003)

J.R. Daeschner, *True Brits* (Arrow Books, 2004)

Uffa Fox, *Joys of Life* (Newnes, 1966)

Hugh Hornby, *Uppies and Downies: The Extraordinary Football Games of Britain* (English Heritage, 2008)

R. Hutton, *The Stations of the Sun – A History of the Ritual Year in Britain* (Oxford University Press, 1996)

Jean Jefferies, *Cheese Rolling in Gloucestershire* (Tempus Publishing, 2007)

Charles Kightly, *The Customs and Ceremonies of Britain – An Encyclopaedia of Living Traditions* (Thames and Hudson, 1986)

Steve Roud, *The English Year* (Penguin, 2006)

Lucinda Wierenga, *Sandcastles Made Simple* (Stewart, Tabori and Chang, 2005)

A.A. Milne, *Winnie-the-Pooh – Complete Collection of Stories and Poems* (Methuen, 2001)

WEBLINKS

http://en.wikipedia.org/wiki/Wiki

http://jrdaeschner.blogspot.com

http://llanwrtyd-wells.powys.org.uk

http://officialpudthrowing.mysite.orange.co.uk

http://swatonvintageday.sslpowered.com/index.html

www.2camels.com

www.3shoes.co.uk

www.ashbourne-town.com

www.atherstone.org.uk

www.bamptonoxon.co.uk/spajers.html

www.barleymowbonsall.co.uk
www.bbc.co.uk
www.bdb.co.za/shackle/articles/throwing_eggs.htm
www.birdman.org.uk
www.bsac.org/news.htm
www.cancerresearchuk.org.uk
www.captaincutlass.com
www.cheese-rolling.co.uk
www.commandochallenge.co.uk
www.cotswolds.info
www.worldcrazygolf.co.uk
www.dartmouthregatta.co.uk
www.dasac.co.uk
www.davespix.co.uk
www.derbyshire-peakdistrict.co.uk
www.doctordanger.com
www.docrowe.org.uk
www.eggthrowing.com
www.egremontcrabfair.org.uk
www.emmawoodphotos.co.uk/blog
www.england-in-particular.info
www.francisfrith.com
www.gawthorpe.ndo.co.uk
www.green-events.co.uk
www.guardian.co.uk
www.hallaton.org/bottlekicking
www.hutc.tv
www.islandsc.org.uk
www.knaresborough.co.uk/bedrace
www.kulicky.com/en
www.lewesarms.org.uk

www.marblemuseum.org.uk

www.mirror.co.uk

www.miniaturegolfer.com

www.mtb-wales.com

www.naddar.org.uk

www.northdevonhospice.org.uk

www.officialpudthrowing.mysite.orange.co.uk

www.olimpickgames.co.uk

www.olneytowncouncil.co.uk/pancake.php

www.otterytarbarrels.co.uk

www.philtaylorphoto.co.uk

www.playedinbritain.co.uk

www.pooh-sticks.com

www.preston.gov.uk

www.royal-oak.uk.com

www.royal-southern.co.uk

www.slsc.org.uk

www.soglos.com

www.stoneskimming.com

www.storytellersofnottingham.co.uk

www.strangebritain.co.uk

www.strawrace.co.uk

www.stupidsteve.co.uk

www.swatonvintageday.sslpowered.com

www.telegraph.co.uk

www.ten80.tv

www.tetburywoolsack.co.uk

www.timetravel-britain.com

www.thebigsheep.co.uk

www.thebottleinn.co.uk

www.thesun.co.uk

www.totnesinformation.co.uk
www.toughguy.co.uk
www.the-tree.org.uk
www.triptojerusalem.com
www.wcpc.me.uk
www.witcham.org.uk
www.wookey.co.uk
www.worldconkerchampionships.com
www.worldcrazygolf.co.uk
www.wormcharming.com
www.xmaspuddingrace.org.uk
www.yarr.org.uk/talk/